Comedians

A PLAY IN THREE ACTS

by Trevor Griffiths

SAMUEL FRENCH, INC.

25 WEST 45TH STREET   NEW YORK 10036
7623 SUNSET BOULEVARD   HOLLYWOOD 90046
LONDON   *TORONTO*

OPENING NIGHT, NOVEMBER 28, 1976

The Music Box

IRVING BERLIN SELECT THEATRES CORPORATION
OWNERS

ALEXANDER H. COHEN
In Association with Gabriel Katzka and Edward L. Schuman

presents

COMEDIANS

by
TREVOR GRIFFITHS

Directed by
MIKE NICHOLS

starring

MILO O'SHEA

JOHN LITHGOW   REX ROBBINS

with

DAVID MARGULIES	**LARRY LAMB**	**JARLATH CONROY**	**JEFFREY DeMUNN**
ROBERT GERRINGER	**NORMAN ALLEN**	**JAYANT BLUE**	**ARMAND ASSANTE**	**WOODY KESSLER**

and

JONATHAN PRYCE

Designed by	*Lighting by*	*Scenery and Costumes Supervised by*
JOHN GUNTER	**RON WALLACE**	**JAMES TILTON**

Co-produced by
HILDY PARKS and **ROY A. SOMLYO**

The Producers wish to express their appreciation to
Theatre Development Fund for its support of the production.

The Producers and Theatre Management are Members
of The League of New York Theatres and Producers, Inc.

THE CAST
(*In Order of Appearance*)

CARETAKER .... *Norman Allen*

GETHIN PRICE .... *Jonathan Pryce*

PHIL MURRAY .... *Jeffrey DeMunn*

GEORGE MCBRAIN .... *Larry Lamb*

SAMMY SAMUELS .... *David Margulies*

MICK CONNOR .... *Jarlath Conroy*

EDDIE WATERS .... *Milo O'Shea*

GED MURRAY .... *John Lithgow*

MR. PATEL .... *Jayant Blue*

BERT CHALLENOR .... *Rex Robbins*

CLUB SECRETARY—M.C. .... *Robert Gerringer*

TEDDY .... *Armand Assante*

PIANIST .... *Woody Kessler*

The play is set in a secondary school and in a workingmen's club in Manchester, England.

Comedians

ACT ONE

A classroom in a secondary school in Manchester, about three miles east of the Centre, on the way to Ashton-under-Lyne and the hills of East Lancashire. Built 1947 in the now disappearing but still familiar two-storey style, the school doubles as evening centre for the area, and will half-fill as the evening progresses with the followers of Yoga, Karate, Cordon Bleu Cookery, 'O' Level English, Secretarial Prelims, Do-It-Yourself, Small Investments and Antique Furniture. Adults will return to school and the school will do its sullen best to accommodate them.

This room, on the ground floor, is smallish, about a dozen chipped and fraying desks, two dozen chairs set out in rows facing the small dais on which stands the teacher's desk, with green blackboard unwiped from the day's last stand beyond. Two starkish lights, on the window side of the room, are on, flintily, lighting about a third of it. A clock (Real: keeping real time for the evening) over the board says 7.27. Cupboards of haphazard heights and styles line the walls, above which the dogged maps, charts, tables, illustrations and notices warp, fray, tear, curl and droop their way to limbo. Windows on the left wall show the night dark and wet.

The School Caretaker, *old, gnarled, tiny, is trying to
sponge recent graffiti from the blackboard, in the
lit segment of the room. He has done away with
the 'F' fairly successfully and now begins on the 'U.'
C,K,O,F,F,N,O,B,H,O,L,E stretch out before him.
He mutters "Dirty buggers" as he sponges.*

Gethin Price *arrives, in wet overcoat, carrying a long
canvas bag and a pint of hot water. He puts
down bag and mug by a desk, removes coat and
shirt, takes shaving tackle from the bag and sits,
in his greying vest, to shave in the tiny mirror he
has propped before him.* Price *wears a flat Lenin-
like cloth or denim hat, which he leaves on.*

Corridor sounds, as people hurry for their classes.
Price *shaves with deft precision, surprisingly
dainty-handed.*

The Caretaker *finishes, catches sight of* Price, *is
startled.*

Caretaker. Are you in here? (Price *looks round,
behind, about, with strange clown-like timing, the
foam gleaming like a mask, brush poised.*)
Price. (*Finally.*) Yeah. (*The* Caretaker *sniffs,
looks for his clipboard and list of classes; scans it.*)
Caretaker. I don't see it.
Price. Been here since January. (*Pause.*) Mr.
Waters . . .
Caretaker. Waters. Oh, him. (*Studying* Price *at
his ablutions.*) What is it, Gents' Hairdressing?
Price. Yeah. Some'at like that.
Caretaker. I thought you practiced on balloons. I
saw it once in a film . . . (*He stumps out dragging*

his waste-bag, pins PHIL MURRAY *to the door as they pass.* MURRAY *in. Stops in doorway as he sees* PRICE'S *foaming white face.*)

PHIL. (*Sour, his dominant note.*) Ee, bloody hell, it's Father Christmas. (PRICE *shaves on, smiling briefly.* MURRAY *carries his two suitcases to a desk and deposits them tidily before sitting down. He's 29, small, dapper, an insurance agent in thick-fitting dark three piece suit.*) Christ, what a flap. God knows where that bloody idiot of a brother of mine's got to. (*He checks his watch against the clock.*) He's probably forgot, the stupid lump. Be having a game o' darts in the New Inn. (*Across to* PRICE.) Are you ready then? (PRICE *grunts yes or no, it makes no matter.*) I am. By God, I am. I've worked meself puce for tonight, I have. I have that. And if that dopey prick . . . (*He leaves it hanging, minatory.* GEORGE McBRAIN *in, straight from work. He's a docknocker, big, beefy, wears an old parka, jeans, boots, shock of black hair, an extrovert Ulsterman in his late thirties.*)

McBRAIN. (*Arms wide in doorway.*) De da! (*Nothing. He looks from* MURRAY *to* PRICE.) Well, I found the latrines, now all I've gotta do is find the classroom. (*Advancing, bag in hand.*) Are we all ready then? Tonight at this club you will see . . . something! Overtime every night this week on those bloody docks but am I worried? Not a bit of it. Because I have what it takes. And when you have it . . . (*He produces a can of Worthington 'E' from his bag on the desk.*) . . . By God you have it!

PHIL. (*To* PRICE.) He sounds as if he's had it for a while too.

McBRAIN. Mock on, Brother. I can forgive your jealousy.

PHIL. (*Grinning slightly.*) You're a big-headed bugger, George, I'll give you that . . .

McBRAIN. (*Strutting, pleased.*) I am that, Mr. Murray. There's not many of us left can walk on water. (PRICE *finishes, replaces shaving tackle, begins to dress.*) How's it going then, Geth?

PRICE. O.K. (*He picks up the mug. Leaves the room.* McBRAIN *slowly follows him halfway, stops, looks at* PHIL MURRAY.)

McBRAIN. Feeling the strain, doubtless.

PHIL. (*Trying a shiny pair of black pointed shoes on.*) Teacher's pet? He's just a moody bugger.

McBRAIN. Where's your brother, then? And where's the bloody rest of 'em? Look at the time . . .

PHIL. Don't ask me about my brother. It's bad enough I have to work with him. I was picking him up on Market Street wasn't I, seven o'clock. *I* was there. Parked in a tow-away zone wasn't I? If *he'd* been there, there'd've been two of us.

(SAMMY SAMUELS *in. He's 41, fat, Manchester Jewish, with cigar, heavy finely cut black overcoat, Homburg, white silk scarf, black attache case.*)

McBRAIN. (*Stan Laurel voice, massaging head with fingers.*) Hi, Olly.

SAMUELS. (*Evenly.*) Piss off. (*He crosses to a desk, carefully removes hat, coat [which he shakes], scarf, and adjusts his shirt cuffs so that the diamond cufflinks do their work below the sleeve of his good wool suit.* MICK CONNOR *in quickly, stops near doorway, rain dripping from his donkey jacket, beneath which we glimpse hired evening dress and crumpled button hole.*)

McBRAIN. Oh, Christ.

CONNOR. Almost, my son. Try again.

McBRAIN. You're drowned. What've you come in your tuxedo for?

CONNOR. They finished us early, down the building site. Thought I'd get it done with. Bloody weather. No pigging buses.

PHIL. You'll look like a dog's dinner.

McBRAIN. (*An explosion.*) Then Ken-L-Ration Kid. Ha! That's good that! I like that! (*Frank Carson voice.*) It's the way I tell 'em. (*The groans of the others increase his glee.*)

SAMUELS. (*Strong Manchester accent, occasional Jewish nasality.*) These pipes are hot, Mick. Get over here and dry out, lad. (CONNOR *crosses to the pipes. We see 'Wimpey' on the PVC patch on the back of the jacket as he removes it.*)

CONNOR. (*Crossing.*) Great bloody weather for ducks, right enough.

PHIL. (*Watching* McBRAIN *opening his tea.*) What she give you this week, George?

McBRAIN. (*Sniffing a sandwich.*) I think it's fish.

PHIL. (*Cadging.*) Nice?

McBRAIN. (*Attacking* PHIL *with one.*) Aye, if you like pirranha.

SAMUELS. (*Seeing the suit jacket.*) Hey, that's not a bad fit. Where'd you gerrit, Woolworth's?

CONNOR. S'matter of fact belonged to a feller I know passed on.

SAMUELS. Not surprised, wearing a suit like that.

CONNOR. What's wrong with the suit? It's a bit wet . . .

SAMUELS. S' hard to put your finger on . . .

McBRAIN. . . . as the actress said to the bishop . . . (*Groan.*)

SAMUELS. (*Studiously contemptuous of the inter-*

ruption.) It's the sort of suit you walk into a tailor's in and ask for the cheapest suit in the shop and he says you're wearing it. (*Groan*.) Don't groan, you scum, learn.

CONNOR. (*Studying the suit*.) S'been a good suit.

SAMUELS. It was doomed the moment it left the animal. Believe me, I know about these things.

PHIL. Christ, he's doing half his bloody act . . .

SAMUELS. Don't worry about me, old son. Plenty more where that came from.

PHIL. That's what I'm bloody worried about . . .

MCBRAIN. Right. Why should Ken Dodd worry about some obscure Manchester Jew stealing his lines? Ha!

SAMUELS. (*He smiles, a little frost around the teeth, at* MCBRAIN.) Why indeed. Why indeed.

CONNOR. (*Aware of that faint crackle*.) Sure it's a detail. A detail it is.

MCBRAIN. (*In* WATERS' *exact voice, assuming his manner*.) Ah, but detail, friend, is all. I'd like you all to remember that now . . . (EDDIE WATERS *in, quick, purposeful, behind* SAMUELS' *back*.)

SAMUELS. Where *is* His Grace, by the way . . . ?

WATERS. He's here. (*There's a small but discernible reaction in the others, a regression to childhood responses. Already within reach of his desk*.) Sorry it's late. I had to check the equipment down at the club. No piano. ("*Bloody hell*"s *of concern*.) It's all right, they've had one sent down from Edge Lane. (*Pause*.) Right, let's get cracking, we haven't got all night. (*He's deposited his gear around the desk, papers, books, a stop watch, other materials and equipment*.) Get the tables sorted and settle yourselves down while I take a leak . . . (*He's on his way back to the door. The others break and begin drawing the desks and*

chairs into roughly parallel sides of a hollow square.
In the doorway he meets PRICE, *returning.* PRICE *has*
removed his hat to reveal an almost shaven skull, the
hair dense and metallic on the scalp. Stopping, staring.)
Mr. Price. (*Over shoulder, very dry.*) Less noise if
you would, gentlemen. There may be people trying to
sleep in other classrooms. (*Back to* PRICE *now, staring
at head.*) All . . . ready?

PRICE. Yeah. Just about, Mr. Waters.

WATERS. (*The head incomprehensible yet unmen-
tionable.*) Still finishing on the song . . . ?

PRICE. I'm not doing a song.

WATERS. How d'you mean? How're you gonna get
off?

PRICE. (*Evasive, stubborn.*) I've er . . . I've bin
working on something else.

WATERS. (*Some faint concern.*) Since when?

PRICE. Oh, last week. I dint like the act. I found
something in the book you lent me.

WATERS. Yes, but you've not changed the basic,
Gethin . . . I mean a week . . .

PRICE. (*Breaking deliberately into the room.*) It'll
be all right, Mr. Waters. (*He takes a desk end with*
PHIL. WATERS *watches him, leaves.*)

McBRAIN. (*To* PRICE.) Hey. (PRICE *looks at him
over his shoulder.*) Love the hairdo.

PRICE. (*Evenly.*) Nice, innit.

PHIL. Joined the skinheads, have we? Gonna smash
a few trains up are you? (PRICE *ignores him.*)

SAMUELS. Reminds me of a girl I used to know. (*Reflective.*) I've known some funny women.

McBRAIN. Reminds me of the wife. After the opera-
tion.

CONNOR. She's had it as well has she?

McBRAIN. Ey, eh . . . (*They square up to each other in mock battle stances.*)

PHIL. Are you shifting these desks or what?

McBRAIN. I heard the Holy Church had granted the Pope a special dispensation . . . to become a nun. (*Beat.*)

CONNOR. That's right. Only on Fridays though. (*They grin, begin humping a desk.*)

PHIL. Look at the time. I'll cut his bloody legs off.

SAMUELS. And he'll still be bigger than you. (*PRICE has taken a tiny violin and large bow from his bag, begins to tune it quietly.*)

McBRAIN. (*Miming M.C. in the cleared central area between the desk.*) Ladies and gentlemen, welcome to the Factory Street Copacabana, where a feast of comedy talent on tonight's bill includes Mr. Sammy Samuels, the Golda Meir of Gagland, hot from his recent sizzling successes in the Gaza Hilton, and not forgetting, of course, the Telly Savalas of comedy, author of the highly acclaimed The Naked Jape, Mr. Gethin . . . What the *hell's* that thing?

PRICE. (*As to a child, slowly.*) This? It's a . . . very, very small . . . violin. Vi. O. Lin. Try it. Vio. Lin.

McBRAIN. Vio. Nil. Vay. Lone. Velo. Line. No. Velo. No. . . .

PRICE. Vio. Lin. Keep practising. It'll come. (*McBRAIN stands blinking, trying to say the word.*)

SAMUELS. Hey. Jack Benny. You're not Jewish.

PRICE. (*Perfect Manchester Jewish, perfect Jack Benny pose.*) You wanna make some kind of a bet, Moishe?

McBRAIN. (*Elated.*) Violin! Got it! Vaseline. Shit!

(WATERS *back in. They sit down at their desks with a muffled clatter and scrape.*)

WATERS. Right, let's see who's here . . . Jack Thomas is out. Tonsilitis.

McBRAIN. Tough. Poor old Jack.

WATERS. What about your brother, Mr. Murray?

PHIL. (*Nervous.*) He'll be here, Mr. Waters. He's probably been held up somewhere.

SAMUELS. Maybe he got a little behind with his milk-round.

CONNOR. I've heard tell it's more than behind these milkmen are after getting. Sure my wife's the only woman in the street our milkman hasn't parked his truck in.

McBRAIN. The stuck-up bitch! (*Laughter.*)

WATERS. (*Dry.*) Oh, we're working tonight, gentlemen. How can they say Music Hall is dead when jokes like that survive . . . down the ages? Right, settle down, we'll make a start. (*Looking at clock.*) Now, we're down at the club at 8.35 or so for a nine o'clock start. That gives us till about twenty five past. And remember we come back here as soon as it's finished, just to round things off and er . . . listen to the verdict. Which brings me to the man they're sending. (*Taking opened envelope from inside pocket, taking letter out.*) His name's . . . Bert Challenor . . . some of you may have heard of him . . . he played the Halls a fair while back, Music Hall, before he took up . . . talent spotting. He'll be here the other side of eight, so you'll get a chance to weigh him up before the off. (*Pause. Scanning them.*) I don't want to say much about him. He's an agent. Which means he's got power. I'd better say this, though: I've never rated him. And he's never thought much of me either.

CONNOR. Sounds a nice chap.

WATERS. Now I'm not saying any of this is going to count against you. But we . . . have our differences. I'd hoped for someone else, to tell truth. (*Puzzled looks, faint consternation.*)

SAMUELS. How do you mean, differences?

WATERS. I don't wanna spend all night on it . . . I never joined his . . . Comedy Artists and Managers Federation, for a start. They took it bad, for some reason. I didn't like what they stood for. I've been a union man all my life, it wasn't that . . . They wanted the market . . . They wanted to control entry into the game. I told 'em no comedian (*Odd, particular emphasis.*) worth his salt could ever 'federate' with a manager. (*Pause, sniff.*) And as far as I'm concerned no comedian ever did . . .

PRICE. (*Very distinctly.*) You think he'd . . . fail us . . . just for that, Mr. Waters, do you?

WATERS. That's not what I said . . .

McBRAIN. Nobody'll fail me. I'm unfailable.

CONNOR. Will you listen to the Pope, now.

PRICE. (*Piercing, within the control.*) Well, what then?

WATERS. Well, put baldly, if I've done a good job with you lot, and he sees it, he won't like it. That's all. (*They look at each other, a trifle more concerned.*)

McBRAIN. (*Reassuring.*) What does it matter, a comic's a comic.

SAMUELS. Not in Mr. Challenor's book he ain't.

WATERS. (*Deliberate.*) Not in Eddie Waters' book either. (*Silence. Some sniffs.*) I probably overstate the problem. You're all good enough . . . now . . . to force his hand, without playing down . . .

McBRAIN. Creme de la creme.

SAMUELS. A little clotted here and there perhaps.

McBRAIN. More there than here, Isaac.

PRICE. (*Sudden.*) Why don't we start?

ALL. Why don't we start? Why don't we start, eh? (*Rather crazily to each other, begin to discuss it.*)

CONNOR. (*Over growing din.*) What an excellent suggestion, give that man a bowler hat for his pains . . .

WATERS. (*Quelling it firmly.*) All right. (*Pause. Silence.*) In the time remaining I thought we might just run through a few exercises to get the blood running . . .

(GED MURRAY *half backs into the room, soaked through. He's large, gentle, direct, open, very far from stupid. Pale, with bad teeth and balding. He wears a milkman's brown coat and hat. He continues, a line at a time, as he makes his way into the room, greets people with winks or smiles, finds his chair, adjusts it, sits down, apparently wholly unaware of the interruption of process he represents. A brilliant comic performance, in other words.*)

GED. (*Taking coat off, shaking it, adjusting himself on the way.*) Sorry I'm late. It's bloody pissing down out there. I fell asleep on the settee watching the Flintstones. So I had to nip down to work and borrow a truck to get here. And t'bloody battery were dead. Got stuck on the Old Road. Walked the last sodding mile. Evening Mr. Waters. (*He hits his seat next to brother* PHIL.) Evening all. (*A big friendly grin.*)

ALL. (*In chorus.*) Good evening, Howdy Doody. (WATERS *waits, a little impatient, for quiet.*)

PHIL. (*Hoarse, hostile.*) I waited ten minutes in a tow-away zone . . .

GED. (*Easily.*) Don't worry, I'm here now.

PHIL. Couldn't you have put something else on?

GED. What's wrong with this?

PHIL. What you watching t'Flintstones for?

GED. It helps me sleep.

WATERS. (*He taps the desk with a piece of chalk.*) If you've nearly finished . . . ?

GED. Sorry, Mr. Waters.

PHIL. (*Suppressed mutter.*) So you bloody should be . . .

CONNOR. (*Setting it up with the others.*) How's the wife then, Ged?

GED. (*Simply.*) Oh, she's all right, thanks . . .

WATERS. (*Dry but permitting.*) Maybe I'm not here . . . (*Some laughter.* GED *indicates his apology facially.*) Right, let's get you warm. A few exercises. (*Points to* McBRAIN, *immediately to his right.*) Character. Stupid.

McBRAIN. (*Fast, in character.*) Excuse me, Miss, where do I put this thing? (*Long pause.*) Oh . . .

WATERS. (*To* SAMUELS, *next.*) Ancient.

SAMUELS. (*Fast, in character.*) Moses? Do I remember Moses? I was with him the day he got the tablets. The Lord said, Anybody want any Commandments? Moses said, How much they going for? The Lord said, They're free. He said, Give us ten.

WATERS. (*To* CONNOR *on end.*) Silly.

CONNOR. Erm . . .

WATERS. Come on, Mick, silly.

CONNOR. (*Drunk Dublin.*) I'll take a pound of sausages with the leaves left on . . . (WATERS *snorts, sustaining the speeded rhythms of the exercise.*)

WATERS. (*To* PRICE, *end of left desk.*) Feminine.

PRICE. (*Fast, perfect.*) Four quid, dearie.

WATERS. (*He stares at him, thrown a little, perhaps by the unexpected harshness.*) Try another.

PRICE. (*Same voice.*) . . . All I said was, all I *said was* . . . four quid doesn't cover sheets . . . Just take your boots off, is that too much to ask?

WATERS. (*To* GED MURRAY, *next.*) Aristocratic.

GED. (*Almost own voice, a strange modification, after thought.*) Could you let me have some clean bread for this bacon grease, Miss . . . ?

WATERS. Nice. (*To* PHIL MURRAY.) Absent-minded.

PHIL. (*Bad Robb Wilton.*) A'll never forget . . .

CONNOR. (*Distinct whisper.*) Whatsisname.

PHIL. Whatsisname. Look, piss off will you, Mick . . . ?

WATERS. O.K. Coming. It's speed . . . and it's detail. But it's the detail inside the speed that makes the difference. A bit sluggish. We'll send it the other way. (*To* PHIL MURRAY.) Willy.

PHIL. Willy Nilly.

GED. Willy Won'ty.

PRICE. Willy Nocomebackagain.

CONNOR. Willy Ell.

SAMUELS. (*Pulling face.*) God Villy . . .

McBRAIN. (*Same face.*) Willy Nands.

WATERS. God. (*To* McBRAIN.) Sammy.

McBRAIN. Sammy . . . ?

WATERS. Yes yes . . .

McBRAIN. (*Desperate.*) Sammy Circle.

WATERS. (*Urgent.*) Right, come on.

SAMUELS. (*Very yiddish.*) Sammyterwidyou?

CONNOR. (*Italian.*) 'Sa me you wanta see? Why dincha say so?

PRICE. Sammykazi (*Pause.*) The Suicidal Shithouse.

GED. (*Singing.*) Sam Enchanted Evening . . .

PHIL. Sammy Professional.

McBrain. Did someone call? I thought I heard my name.

Waters. Not bad. Let's stretch it a bit. (*Stopwatch.*) You've got a cougher in the audience down at the club tonight. Let's see how you deal with a cough. Any order, off you go.

McBrain. (*Fluent.*) By, she's coughing well tonight. What've you been doing to her, eh? Dirty thing, you.

Samuels. (*Jumping in.*) There's an old Indian remedy for coughing in women, you know. Full of spices and herbs and other Asian comestibles. It's a sort of curry linctus . . . (*Groans all round.*) They say it's very good . . . (Waters *stares at him, stone-faced.*)

Price. (*In fast. Perfectedly acted.*) Do you realize, we're all sharing the same air with that man. Just listen to him. (*Waits.*) Every time he does that there's a million infectious droplets joins the pool. He's emptying his lungs over everyone here. Go on, empty away son, we don't mind . . .

Connor. I tell you what, why don't you come up here and cough and we'll all sit down there and laugh at you . . .

McBrain. Mek a change for *your* act, Mick.

Ged. I think she's trying to tell me something.

Phil. Yeah, you're rubbish.

Ged. Oh you speak the language do you? That's nice.

Phil. Yes, I learnt it at school.

Ged. Oh they dint teach us out like that. They just taught us spittin'. And peein' up walls . . .

Phil. Ay well, that's the special school for you intit. S'just a bad system . . .

McBrain. Cough and the world coughs with you. Fart and you stand alone.

WATERS. (*Tough.*) All right . . .

PRICE. (*He is already climbing up onto his desk.*) There was a young lady called Hunt . . .

MCBRAIN. Yes, yes . . .

PRICE. Who had a remarkable stunt . . .

CONNOR. No, no.

PRICE. With a frightening cough . . .

SAMUELS. Yes.

PRICE. She would jerk herself off . . .

MCBRAIN. Ah . . .

PRICE. (*Vicious but quiet.*) By sinking her teeth in her cunt.

ALL. Ole! (WATERS *stares at him. The others laugh, puzzled yet amused.*)

CARETAKER. (*From doorway.*) Smoking is not allowed on these premises. Thank you. (*He turns again.*) Or standing on desks. Or anything else like that. (*He leaves with dignity.* PRICE *gets down, white, impassive, avoiding* WATERS' *eyes, which follow him, close and tense as he resumes his seat.*)

WATERS. (*Quiet, still.*) Is somebody trying to tell me something? (*Pause.*) Mmm? (*No answer.* PRICE *twangs a tiny violin string, once, twice, three times. Slight tense sense of discomfiture as they try to locate his meaning.*) The traitor distrusts the truth (*They look at him.*) The traitor distrusts the truth. Tongue twisters. Shall we twist tongues, gentlemen? (*They take it up in turn. Calls.*) Faster. (*The phrase gradually loses its shape and meaning in the struggle for facility.* WATERS *sends it down* MCBRAIN'S *line first, then* PHIL MURRAY'S *so that we end on* PRICE.)

PRICE. (*Effortlessly, at speed.*)
The traitor distrusts the truth.
The traitor distrusts the truth.
The traitor distrusts the truth.

The traitor distrusts the truth.
The traitor distrusts the truth.
The traitor distrusts the truth.
The traitor distrusts the truth.
(*Long pause. Very levelly, measuredly, at* WATERS.)
The traitor distrusts the truth.

WATERS. (*Finally; mild, matter-of-fact, reflective.*)
I've never liked the Irish, you know. Dr. Johnson said
they were a very truthful race, they never spoke well
of each other, but then how could they have? (*They
look around, faintly puzzled, amused.*) Big, thick,
stupid heads, large cabbage ears, hairy nostrils, daft
eyes, fat, flapping hands, stinking of soil and Guinness.
The niggers of Europe. Huge, uncontrollable wangers,
spawning their degenerate kind wherever they're allowed to settle. I'd stop them settling here if I had my
way. Send 'em back to the primordial bog they came
from. Potato heads. (*Pause.* McBRAIN *clenches and un-
clenches his fists on the desk, watches them carefully.*)

CONNOR. (*Slowly.*) Would that be Southern Irish or
Northern Irish, Mr. Waters?

WATERS. (*Mildly on.*) Or Jews, for that matter.

SAMUELS. What are you staring at me for? (*Uneasy
laughter, dying fast.*)

WATERS. (*Still very matter-of-fact, reflecting still.*)
They have this *greasy* quality, do Jews. Stick to their
own. Grafters. Fixers. Money. Always money. Say
Jews, say gold. Moneylenders, pawnbrokers, usurers.
They have the nose for it, you might say. Hitler put
it more bluntly: "If we do not take steps to maintain
the purity of blood, the Jew will destroy civilization
by poisoning us all." The effluent of history. Scarcely
human. Grubs.

SAMUELS. (*Unfunnily.*) He must've met the wife's
family.

WATERS. Negroes. Cripples. Defectives. The Mad. Women. (*Turning deliberately to* MURRAY'S *row.*) Workers. Workers. Dirty, unschooled. Shifty. Grabbing all they can get. Coal in the bath. Chips with everything. Chips and beer. Trade Unions dedicated to maximizing wages and minimizing work. Strikes for the idle. Their greed. And their bottomless stupidity. Like children, unfit to look after themselves. Breeding like rabbits, sex-mad. And their mean, vicious womenfolk, driving them on. Animals, to be fed slops and fastened up at night. (*Long pause.*) The traitor destroys the truth. (*Silence. Coughing. Shuffling of feet.*)

PRICE. Gone very dark in here all of a sudden. (*Silence again.*)

McBRAIN. Fancy a hand of cards? (*Silence again.* WATERS *looks down at his desk. They exchange enquiring looks across his space.*)

GED. (*Finally.*) I don't get that. (*Pause.*) Were it some kind of a joke, Mr. Waters?

WATERS. Not exactly a joke, Mr. Murray.

GED. I mean. There's good and bad in everyone, int there . . .

WATERS. Is there now?

CONNOR. Didn't you say so yourself?

WATERS. Did I?

SAMUELS. You're always saying it. "A comedian draws pictures of the world. The closer you look, the better you'll draw." (*In the silence that follows, a penny begins to drop.*)

PRICE. (*Laconic, drawn out.*) Lesson Three: "Stereotypes." (*Some faint embarrassment, the sense, however obscure, of having let* WATERS *down.*)

SAMUELS. You *were* putting us on. That's a relief. I

was beginning to get a bit worried. (*Some relaxation, smiles, off the hook.*)

WATERS. (*Driving home.*) If I've told you once I've told you a thousand times. We work *through* laughter, not *for* it. If all you're about is raising a laugh, OK, get on with it, good luck to you, but don't waste my time. There's plenty others as'll tek your money and do the necessary. Not Eddie Waters.

McBRAIN. (*Conciliatory, apologetic.*) So, a few crappy jokes, Mr. Waters . . .

WATERS. It's not the jokes. It's not the jokes. It's what lies behind 'em. It's the attitude. A comedian— that's a daring man. He dares to see what his listeners shy away from, fear to express. And what he sees is a sort of truth, about people, about their situation, about what hurts or terrifies them, about what's hard, above all, about what they *want*. Any joke releases the tension. But a true joke, a comedian's joke, has to do more than release tension, it has to *liberate* the will and the desire, it has to *change the situation*. (*Pause.*) And when a joke bases itself upon a distortion— (*At* PRICE, *deliberately.*) a "stereotype" perhaps—and gives the lie to the truth so as to win a laugh and stay in favour, we've moved away from a comic art and into the world of "entertainment" and "success." (*Pause.*) You're better than that, damn you. And even if you're not, you should bloody well want to be.

CONNOR. (*Slowly, trying to follow the argument.*) I want to be famous. I want to be rich and famous. What's wrong with that, Mr. Waters?

WATERS. More than you want to be good?

McBRAIN. What's wrong with being all three?

WATERS. Nothing. So long as you're good *first*. Because you'll never be good later.

PRICE. (*Suddenly.*) Was it my limerick?

WATERS. I don't want to personalize this discussion . . .

PRICE. Oh, I see. You think talking to the six of us makes it impersonal do you . . . ?

PHIL. Oh, come on, Pricey, don't argue . . .

PRICE. Why not? He's accusing us . . . me . . . of doing some'at . . . immoral, I want to know what he means, it's pretty important to me . . .

SAMUELS. Look, we don't want a scene . . .

PRICE. Who wants a scene? I put a simple question. I'm just looking for a "truth" . . . Was it my limerick he took objection to? (*Pause.*) Because if it was, I'd like to know what his objections are, that's all.

SAMUELS. Well just don't push your luck, O.K.?

GED. (*Gentle, but firm.*) It's not up to you, Sammy.

WATERS. All right. (*They're quiet.*) Let's hear it again, Mr. Price.

PRICE. What?

WATERS. Will you recite it for us?

PRICE. What for?

WATERS. Give us a chance to look it over, see what we're dealing with.

PRICE. It was it then, was it?

WATERS. *You* think it was.

SAMUELS. Let's hear it then.

PHIL. Yeah, let's hear it. (*Pause.* PRICE *bites his lip, sullen, moody.* WATERS *waits.*)

PRICE. (*Slowly.*) All right.
There was a young lady called Hunt
Who had a remarkable stunt
With a frightening cough
She would jerk herself off
By sinking her teeth in her cunt. (*Silence.*)

WATERS. It's clever. Is it your own?

PRICE. You could say that.

WATERS. How do you mean?

PRICE. I made it up. Just then.

WATERS. It's very clever.

GED. (*Marveling.*) You never made it up. Did you?

PRICE. Look, Mr. Waters, I don't want compliments, just say what you don't like and we can get on . . .

WATERS. What do you think it says?

PRICE. I don't know. You tell me. I felt like saying it.

WATERS. (*Crossing to board, chalking up key words one beneath another; fast in monotone.*) Hunt. Hunt says cunt. Lady, cunt. Cunt, bad word, unsayable. Might say it, going to say it, got to say it, Stunt, fooled you, build the suspense, cough, cough, jerked herself off, women masturbate, naughty, must say it new, dadadadadadadada *cunt. There!*

PRICE. So?

WATERS. It's a joke that hates women, Gethin.

PRICE. How come?

WATERS. It's a joke that hates women *and* sex. (*Aware of the danger.*) Do I go on?

PRICE. (*Cool, daring him.*) Why not?

WATERS. (*Taking it somewhere safer.*) In the Middle Ages men called the woman's sexual organ the devil's mark. According to Freud, men still see them as shark's mouths, in dreams. When you walk into that arena with a joke, you've gotta know why you're there.

PRICE. Maybe I'm just frightened.

WATERS. Maybe. But who do you blame, with your joke? Your lady 'jerks herself off.' Is she a man?

PRICE. It rhymes with cough.

WATERS. *Off* rhymes with cough. What do you *think* of your lady?

PRICE. Not a lot.

WATERS. Acrobatic but nasty? Sex-starved? Sex-mad? A nympho. Sexually insatiable.

McBRAIN. Can I say something?

WATERS. By all means.

McBRAIN. (*Hesitant, conciliatory.*) I mean, I do take your point and that, but doesn't his rhyme do just what you said you wanted? If fellers fear women and sex and that the way you say . . . doesn't that wee rhyme of his kind of . . . liberate the fear, sort of?

WATERS. I don't think it does, George. I think it recognizes it and *traps* it. Leaves it exactly where it is. Doesn't help it on. Doesn't do anything to *change* it. (*To everyone.*) Look, this is probably the last chance I'll get, and I want to state it as simply as I can.

(*The door opens and an* ASIAN *enters, soaked and gleaming, small, slim, dark, delicate, a large muslin-wrapped something under his arm. He stops, smiles, shyly, wavers. They turn to look at him. He leaves, closing the door behind him.* WATERS *crosses to the door after a moment, looks out down the corridor.*)

SAMUELS. (*Sotto voce.*) If that's Challenor, we're all done for.

WATERS. (*He returns to his desk.*) A joke that feeds on ignorance . . . (*Points to* McBRAIN.)

McBRAIN. Starves its audience.

WATERS. We have the choice. We can say something or we can say nothing. Not everything true is funny, and not everything funny is true. Most comics *feed* prejudice and fear and blinkered vision, but the best ones, the comedians . . . illuminate them, make them clearer to see, easier to deal with. We've got to make people laugh . . . (*Pointing at* GED.)

GED. Till they cry.

WATERS. Cry. Till they find their pain and their beauty. Comedy is medicine. Not coloured sweeties to rot the teeth with. (*The* ASIAN *reappears in the doorway.*) Can I help you?

ASIAN. Please, Learning to Read?

WATERS. No . . .

ASIAN. Please. (*He puts down his parcel, fishes a leaflet from his sodden overcoat, hands it to* WATERS. WATERS *studies it, turns it over to read the other side.*) Learning to Read.

WATERS. (*Reading.*) "Reading to Learn."

ASIAN. No. Learning to Read.

WATERS. No, it says Reading to Learn. (*He shows him.*) Reading. To. Learn. (*The* ASIAN *is perplexed.*) "A class in literary appreciation for intending students of the Open University. BBC." I'm no wiser than you, really . . .

ASIAN. A man gave it to me in the Library . . .

WATERS. Aye, well he probably had a sense of humour.

ASIAN. Perhaps somewhere else . . . ?

WATERS. (*Glancing at clock, then decisive.*) Look, I'll take you up to the Principal, he'll sort you out . . . (*He leads him towards door.*) I won't be a minute. Try and sort out the running order while I'm away, will you, George. Look at you, you're soaked, man, how far've you come . . . ? (*They leave.*)

SAMUELS. (*Standing, lighting cigar.*) What a screw up *this* is! (*At* PRICE.) Why don't you keep your bloody trap shut, eh?

McBRAIN. Come on, Sammy.

SAMUELS. Sod off. I want to think about me act, not

arse the night away on . . . philosophy! Especially after he tells us we've got a bent adjudicator.

PHIL. Me too.

CONNOR. I thought you said you couldn't care less whether you did well or not tonight.

SAMUELS. (*Terse.*) Well I do.

CONNOR. With having your own club and that.

GED. (*Winking at* CONNOR.) Yeah. You said you could always employ yourself.

SAMUELS. Listen, cretin, do you wanna know something, I wouldn't be seen dead working a club like mine, I want the top. I want TV, I want the Palladium. *You* can work my club, I'll book *you* as soon as you're ready, you're just what they need. As for that little bastard . . . (*Points at* PRICE, *turns away angrily. Silence.*)

McBRAIN. There was this poacher, see. And he shoots this deer. Big un. Hatstands in its head an' that. And he puts it over his back—like that—and he's hunking it off through the forest when this gamekeeper catches him and says, 'Hey, you're poaching' and your man says 'How do you mean?' and he says 'You've got a deer on your back,' and he looks over his shoulder and he says 'Get off.' (*They laugh, more at the telling than the tale,* PRICE *gets up, steps onto the rostrum, becoming, in the movement, uncannily, the 70 year old* WATERS.)

PRICE. Now, Mr. McBrain, you must see that that joke is totally supportive of all forms of blood sports. Besides which it undoubtedly hints at the dark secret of animal sodomy or, at the very least, the stealthy sodomizing of men by beasts of the field and forest. A *comedian*, George, a comedian would have carried all this out into the open where we could all see it . . . (*He looks for it.*) . . . so that we'd all come to realise what should've been obvious from the start, or the Middle Ages, whichever you prefer, George: namely, deep down, all we want is stuffing up the bum by antlered beasties. (*Pause.*) It's a joke that hates *deer*, George. (McBRAIN, CONNOR *and* PHIL MURRAY *laugh.* SAMUELS *scowls a bit in his corner.*)

GED. (*Serious.*) That's not so funny.

PRICE. (*Sombre.*) No. I suppose it isn't.

McBRAIN. Why've you got it in for him then?

CONNOR. Yeah, what's that about? His favourite an' all. I thought you rated him.

PRICE. I don't want telling what to think. That's all. I don't want telling what to feel.

SAMUELS. You'd've felt my bleeding boot up your bleeding hole if you'd talked that way to me. Look at the bleeding time . . .

PRICE. (*Quiet, with great, inquiring grace.*) I didn't know you was Irish, Sammy . . .

SAMUELS. (*He laughs, a little slow splutter in spite of himself.*) You're a slippy bleeder. Do you know that?

PRICE. (*Rolling eyes.*) Yes, baas. I know that, baas. Yessuh baas. Whup ma hahd an cawl me kinky.

McBRAIN. Answer the question. Why're you so bent on riling the old man. *He's* no different.

PRICE. So maybe I am. (*He strokes his cropped head, an unconscious gesture.*)

CONNOR. Yeah. Maybe it's more than your hairs you've been losing. (PRICE *turns away, smiling.*) I'll tell you something. He's a good old man. And he's a comedian to his toenails. He doesn't *need* to do this for peanuts, you know, every Friday night, *here*, on two quid an hour or whatever it is. He could take a room in a pub and charge a fortune and he'd get it too. So that he can teach pricks like us he does it. (*Pause.*)

And if I get out of the building trade and earn a living doing what I want to do more than anything else, always have done, I'll have him to thank and no one else. (*Deliberately.*) And that goes for everyone here, whether they know it or not.

GED. It goes for me.

McBRAIN. Goes for me too.

PHIL. (*Sourer.*) All right, he's a genius, what is this, Gala Night at the City Varieties?

GED. *We* knew next to nothing.

PHIL. Speak for yourself. I'd worked clubs.

GED. Oh aye. Two. Ardwick and Oldham. One of 'em withheld your money. The other called a taxi to drive you off to safety. (CONNOR *and* McBRAIN *laugh.*)

PHIL. Like the bloody wild west, both of 'em. There was nothing wrong with *me*. My troubles started when I took you on, believe me.

GED. (*Quiet, toughly serious.*) When are you gonna face it: you're not funny. You're a straight. You can't work on your own. (*Pause.*) But *I* can.

PHIL. Try it.

GED. Maybe I will.

McBRAIN. Frying tonight, by God! Jees, listen to 'em go. All of 'em. Those poor bloody guinea pigs of an audience at this club'll know the meaning of tears tonight, by Christ, won't they just. Come on, let's get the order decided, who wants to go first? Sammy? How about you?

SAMUELS. No chance.

McBRAIN. Anyone? (*Nobody.*) O.K. (*Takes pack of cards from his pocket, cuts it twice.*) Lowest loses, aces high. Take a card, ladies. (*They draw cards, peer at them and at each others.*)

CONNOR. (*Last to draw.*) Shit.

McBRAIN. (*Laughing.*) You Mick? Tough.

CONNOR. Ah well. At least they'll be awake.

SAMUELS. Aye, well try and leave 'em that way, will you.

McBRAIN. Second, Sammy?

SAMUELS. All right.

McBRAIN. Ged? Phil?

GED. O.K.

McBRAIN. (*Looking at* PRICE.) How would you feel about going last, Gethin?

PRICE. All the same to me.

McBRAIN. Right. Top of the bill, kidda. Will they be waiting for you! Now, who wants music? (*They show;* McBRAIN *writes it down.*) Gethin, you have music, don't you?

PRICE. No.

McBRAIN. I thought you got off with that wee song. What was it . . .

PRICE. No, I've changed it. No music.

SAMUELS. You're a cool sod, I'll give you that. The bleeding nerve of it, working up an act for three months and then half an hour before he goes on he changes it! You'll come a right cropper one day, you will. I can feel it in me water.

PRICE. (*Deliberately.*) Well, piss over somebody else for a change, Sammy.

McBRAIN. (*Whistling, a perfect football referee.*) Hey, hey, hey, any more of that and you'll go in the book . . . (*He brandishes a book in his right hand.* WATERS *in, followed by the* ASIAN. WATERS *carries a tray with eight teas in plastic cups, spoons, sugar.*)

WATERS. I got the teas in. (*They move towards the tray.*) Gentlemen, this is Mr. Patel.

GED. Hello, Mr. Patel. (*A few more grunts of acknowledgement.*)

McBRAIN. Hey, if you've got any good jokes, I'll

have a word with you before you go . . . (PATEL *smiles innocently.*)

WATERS. Mr. Patel is going to stay with us for a while, I've promised him a lift into town on the way down to the Club. He's, erm . . . he's been sent on a wild goose chase . . . and the monsoon is still with us, as you'll no doubt have observed for yourselves. Sit there if you would, Mr. Patel, by the pipes. Take your coat off if you like.

PATEL. (*Sitting.*) Thank you no sir. I'm very comfortable . . . (WATERS *resumes the desk, picks up* McBRAIN's *list.*)

McBRAIN. That's the order.

WATERS. Fine. And the asterisks are music, yes?

McBRAIN. Ahunh. (WATERS *stares in* PRICE's *direction for a moment, pockets the paper.*)

WATERS. (*At clock.*) I don't want anything from your acts from now on, all right. Just let them lie and get yourselves limber. O.K. Close your eyes. Come on, close your eyes. (*They close their eyes, frowning or amused.*) Now think. Think about yourselves. What you've been, what you've done, what you are, what you want. All right? Keep thinking. Now, take one incident, anything, any little thing, that means something to you, maybe something that embarrasses you or haunts you or still makes you frightened, something you still can't deal with maybe, all right? Now think about it. It may be some'at very gentle, very tender, some'at you said, some'at you did, wanted to do . . . All right. Open up. (*They blink at each other.*)

GED. Bloody hell fire, I were just gettin' into that.

WATERS. Let's hear it then, Mr. Murray.

GED and OTHERS. What?

WATERS. I want you to tell it. In your own way, in your own time. (*Pause.*) But make it funny.

GED. Jesus wept!

SAMUELS. He must have seen your act.

GED. I were thinking about my wife.

McBRAIN. Haha. Very good, very good. It's the way he tells 'em you know. (*He laughs genuinely, full of pleasure.*)

WATERS. (*Softly.*) You're next, George. (*To* GED.) So tell us about it. Be funny. Try.

GED. (*Standing.*) The wife went in hospital, have the kiddie. Ancoats. 'Bout two in the morning. He musta lay there best part of a year, all snug like, planning it just for that moment. I rang up from work next morning about half-five. Nothing. Seven, nothing. Half-nine. Half-ten. I musta bin nervous, I found mesel smoking me own fags. I went to our mother's dinner time, for company I suppose. I know it weren't for t'food. (*Difficult now.*) Me dad'd been off work for a while, Clayton Aniline . . . he'd had a sorts breakdown. (*He touches his head.*) . . . gone a bit queer in the head . . .

PHIL. (*Embarrassed, sotto.*) Bloody hell, what you talkin' about that for . . . ?

GED. Anyroad. I rang again and they said she'd had it so I got a bus and went down. (*Pause.*) When I got to the ward, I couldn't go in.

CONNOR. The door was locked.

GED. I suddenly thought, what if it runs in the family.

McBRAIN. Like crabs, you mean.

GED. No. I thought, what if there's something wrong with it. (*Silence now, the story rivets.*) She were holding it in her arm. I saw it ten beds away. Black hair. Red face. Little fists banging away on wife's face.

(*Pause.*) He were bloody perfect. He were bloody perfect. (*He looks around, unembarrassed, largely unaware of his effect. Some coughs, stirrings, sniffs.*)

PHIL. (*Mutter.*) What you talkin' about that for?

GED. (*Simply.*) I were thinkin' about it.

PHIL. You were thinking about it. Jesus wept.

McBRAIN. I'm not following that, Mr. Waters. No chance.

PRICE. I went nutty once.

SAMUELS. (*Queer.*) Well, you do surprise me, Gethin.

WATERS. Is that what you were thinking about?

PRICE. Sort of.

WATERS. Go on.

PRICE. (*Standing.*) I thumped a teacher.

CONNOR. Oh you're a terrible hard bastard.

PRICE. (*Simply.*) Not really. Were a woman. She called us a guttersnipe. In Music. I clocked her one. It seemed the only thing I could do. She went white. Whiter than me even. Then she cried. Little tears. They sent me to a psychologist. Thirteen. Me I mean, *he* were a bit older. Though not much. We developed a sort of tolerant hatred of each other. He kept on insisting on treating me as an equal, you know, patronizing me. The last time I saw him he gave me this long piece and he said, "You see, Gethin, basically all any of us want is to be loved." And I said, "If you know so much, how come you wear a toupee?" (*Pause.*) That's when I decided I'd be a comedian. (*He sniffs, twangs the violin string, sits.*)

GED. That's about as funny as mine.

PHIL. Yeah, laugh a minute.

WATERS. It's hard isn't it. Not exactly standing in line to go, are we, gentlemen? (*He scans* McBRAIN's *row, then stares at* GED MURRAY.) Why *is* that, do you think? It wouldn't have been *all* waste, Mr. Murray, if your child had been born defective, would it? I mean, it would at least have afforded us a worthy subject for the comic's wit. (*Pause.*) Do we fear . . . other people . . . so much that we must mark *their* pain with laughter, our own with tears? People deserve respect because they're people, not because they are known to us. Hate your audience and you'll end up hating yourself. All right. We'll stop it there . . . (*Look at clock: about 8:20.*) Any final queries about your spots? George? Sammy? (*Both give negatives.*) Mick?

CONNOR. (*Fiddling.*) Y'aven't a dickie have you, this one keeps fallin' off . . . ?

WATERS. I'll have a look at it in the van going down. Gethin? (PRICE *shakes his head.*) Sure? (PRICE *nods.*) What about you two?

PHIL. We're fine, Mr. Waters.

WATERS. (*To everyone.*) I want to wish you luck. You worked hard, you've sweated, you've been honester than most. I'll be pulling for you all tonight. And you'll *know* if you're good. You'll not need tellin'.

(CHALLENOR *knocks, enters on the knock. He's maybe five years younger than* WATERS, *rather waxen, discreetly dressed, with a homburg, and umbrella, which he shakes. His self-regard is almost a mannerism, though he retains a residual lithe charm.*)

CHALLENOR. Evening, Eddie. I'll never understand why they don't run boats to Manchester.

WATERS. We're waiting on the word from London. Hello, Bert.

CHALLENOR. Spry as ever. Eddie Waters, the Lancashire Lad.

WATERS. Relax. You'll see forty, don't you fret.

CHALLENOR. I thought you'd have taken the bungalow at Southport by now, Eddie.

WATERS. Nay. I'm a Manchester man. I'd miss the rain. (*The relaxed yet glinting spat ends.*)

CHALLENOR. These your lads, then?

WATERS. Aye. Mr. Challenor of the C.A.M.F., Phil and Ged Murray, Gethin Price, Mick Connor, Sammy Samuels, George McBrain.

CHALLENOR. How do you do. (*He's looking in* PATEL's *direction, inquiringly.*)

WATERS. Not part of the class.

CHALLENOR. No? There's one or two about, you know. Midland clubs. Awful lot of people, of course . . .

WATERS. Is there anything you want to say before we get down there?

CHALLENOR. (*Checking watch.*) I wouldn't mind a word or two, Eddie. Is it far?

WATERS. No. No. Ten minutes.

(*The* CARETAKER *comes in. He carries a shattered lectern.*)

CARETAKER. (*To* WATERS.) I told the Principal you were looking for him. (*He points in* PATEL's *direction.*) He's back now. He had to go down to the other centre in Beswick. (*He makes a drinking sign with his right hand.*)

WATERS. Thank you, I think we can manage now . . .

CARETAKER. I told him you were looking. He's in his office. Waiting.

WATERS. It's very good of you.

CARETAKER. (*Looking at top of lectern, pulling one piece from the other.*) They've gone bloody *mad* down there, that karate lot. (*He leaves.*)

CHALLENOR. (*He looks at* WATERS.) Don't mind me, Eddie.

WATERS. (*He doesn't want to leave, can't show it.*) We'll go and see the Principal, Mr. Patel, just to make sure you *are* in the wrong place. (PATEL *crosses behind him to the door. To class.*) I'll be back. (*They leave.* CHALLENOR *mounts the dais carefully, stands at the tall, sloping desk, places his black attache case on the ledge.*)

CHALLENOR. Going to give me a good show then?

McBRAIN. That we are. Creme de la creme. You'll laugh tonight, Mr. Challenor, that you will.

CHALLENOR. That's good news, brother. It's been a particularly unfunny day.

SAMUELS. Your worries are over, Mr. Challenor, mark my words. Five of the finest comedy acts East of Liverpool. I'm *very* funny.

CHALLENOR. I'll watch out for you.

SAMUELS. Gate two. Put your money on it.

PHIL. I saw you at the Hulme Hippodrome just after the war, about 1951. Frank Randle top of the bill. Bert Challenor, the Cockney Character.

CHALLENOR. Right. Played Number Ones for twenty years, right through to the end. History to you lot . . .

PRICE. Did you really play with Frank Randle?

CHALLENOR. I did.

PRICE. What were he like? Were he one of the best?

CHALLENOR. Best of his kind, I suppose.

PRICE. How do you mean, of his kind?

CHALLENOR. He was *local*, wasn't he. South of Birmingham he was nothing. A whole set of 'em—Sandy Powell, Albert Modley, Jimmy James. George was the great one. He's the one to study, if you're keen to get on.

PRICE. George Formby?

CHALLENOR. Ahunh.

CONNOR. Didn't Mr. Waters work with your man Formby before the war?

CHALLENOR. Eddie did a lot of things before the war.

SAMUELS. Was he good? (*Pause.*)

CHALLENOR. He was brilliant.

SAMUELS. Yeah? What happened then?

CHALLENOR. (*Quietly.*) He didn't want enough. I don't know. He just . . . stayed up here . . . (*Pause.*)

PRICE. Have you seen Frank Randle's films? I've seen 'em all. He's untouchable, in my book. (*He gets up suddenly, assumes an uncanny Frank Randle stance and gait.*) "I'm as full as vim as a butcher's dog—I'm as lively as a cricket. Baaa, I'll sup it if it keeps me up all neet. I'll take anybody on of my age and weight, dead or alive, and I'll run 'em, walk 'em, jump'em, fight 'em, aye, and I'll play 'em dominoes. Baaa, I've supped some stuff toneet. Listen, ony t'other day I went to a funeral, I were stood at graveside, a chap looked at me, he said, How old are yer? I said 72, how old are you? He said I'm 84, I said, Eeh, I don't think it's much use you going home at all." (*The group laugh.* CHALLENOR *smiles thinly, undazzled.*)

CHALLENOR. Try it in London, sonnie. Try it in Birmingham even.

PHIL. Pay him no heed, Mr. Challenor.

SAMUELS. He argues like other people breathe.

CHALLENOR. Well. Nice meeting you. Good luck for tonight. (*He dwells, enjoying the attention.*) A couple of . . . hints. Don't try to be deep. Keep it simple. I'm not looking for philosophers, I'm looking for comics. I'm looking for someone who sees what the people want and knows how to give it them. It's the people pay the bills, remember, yours, mine . . . Mr. Water's. We're servants, that's all. They demand, we supply. Any good comic can lead an audience by the nose. But only in the direction they're going. And that direction is, quite simply . . . escape. We're not missionaries, we're suppliers of laughter. That's what I'm here to sign up. I'd like you all to remember that. See you down there. Oh. A text for tonight. Perhaps we can't all be Bob Hope. But we can try. (*He takes his leave. Silence.* McBRAIN *opens another two cans of 'E', hands one to* CONNOR. SAMUELS *lights a panatella. They sit looking at each other, scanning for concern or alarm.*)

SAMUELS. (*Disgust staining his voice.*) Oh, that's marvellous. That's . . . marvellous.

PHIL. (*Backing his chair to the floor savagely as he stands.*) Jesus Chirst! What the hell are we gonna do?

SAMUELS. We're gonna get the bum's rush, that's what we're gonna do.

McBRAIN. Not at all. What're you on about?

SAMUELS. Look, you heard him, Seamus . . .

McBRAIN. (*Thinking, already doubtful.*) He had to say that. He's an old enemy of the Boss's, what else could he say?

PHIL. Sod that, what're we gonna *do?*

GED. What's that supposed to mean? We're gonna do our act.

PHIL. He'll murder us. You must be joking.

McBRAIN. That's very nearly funny.

GED. (*To* PHIL, *standing heavily.*) Look, what are you talking about?

PRICE. (*Piercing through the Din.*) He means . . . do you not? . . . how can you change your act at this short notice to suit Challenor. Isn't that what you mean? (*He takes in the whole group in the silence that follows the question. People sniff, shuffle, look at others.*)

SAMUELS. (*Finally.*) It's not such a tragedy. I can paste some'at together. Fortunately, I've managed to keep my distance . . .

CONNOR. Challenor'll get the act I came with. He don't bother me.

SAMUELS. OK, so be the building trade's funniest shit-shoveller, then.

CONNOR. (*Steely; distinct.*) I do not shovel shit, Sammy. All right?

GED. We've got an act . . .

PHIL. We've got several acts. What about the one we used last Christmas?

GED. What? You heard what Mr. Waters thought of that . . .

PHIL. Look Ged, I mean, look, sod Mr. Waters, I don't intend to spend the rest of my days going door to door collecting insurance money. Now I don't. All right?

GED. (*Implacable.*) I don't care what you do or don't do tomorrow. Tonight, we do the act.

PHIL. Do we.

GED. We do.

PHIL. You're stupid.

GED. (*Dangerous, very swift.*) No, Phil. Leave it. (PRICE *watches them all from a distance, limbering up.*)

SAMUELS. What about you George?

MCBRAIN. Oh, I'll think of something. Well known you know for my flexibility. In any case (*Frank Carson.*) it's the way I tell 'em.

PHIL. (*Splenetic.*) If you hate those bloody docks as much as you claim, you'll know what to do all right.

SAMUELS. Somebody shoulda told Challenor they *do*

run boats to Manchester. So that schmucks like you can unload 'em.

McBrain. (*Simply.*) I know what to do. Trust Georgey.

Samuels. (*Pause.* Samuels *turns to* Price.) Whorrabout you then? (Price *is doing left-leg squats. Stops carefully. Swivels gracefully round.*)

Price. (*Innocent.*) Me?

Samuels. *You,* you slippy sod.

Price. (*Distinctly.*) The traitor distrusts the truth. The traitor distorts the truth. The traitor destroys the truth. (Phil *knocks a chair off a desk, enraged still.*)

Samuels. You're dafter than you think, you know.

Price. (*Inward.*) I drive a van all day for British Rail. And if Challenor were on fire I wouldn't piss him out. Bob Hope! (*The venom muscles his throat.*)

McBrain. (*Quietly.*) Maybe you won't have to? (Price's *raised eyebrows ask the question.*) You've changed your act already, haven't you? Who's a clever boy then?

Samuels. (*Sourly marvelling.*) Slippy.

(*Silence* Ged *frowns concern.* Connor *watches.* McBrain *chuckles.* Samuels *clicks his teeth.* Phil Murray *flops back in chair.* Price *stands a moment longer, then moves in for his gear, gathers it, turns, begins to leave.*)

Price. See you at the show, darlings . . . (*He's gone, out on amazing tiptoe, like a dancer in a minefield.*)

Samuels. (*Following slowly to door.*) Waters musta mentioned Challenor, told him last week, after the lesson. They allus have a drink together in the Mare . . .

CONNOR. (*Far from content.*) Forget it, for Christ's sake. Who cares about bloody Challenor . . . (*He gathers his things roughly, angrily: leaves. The others begin to gather their belongings.* WATERS *back in. He carries six buttonholes in plastic bags. Looks at depleted company.*)

WATERS. Ah, the others have gone on, have they . . . I brought one of these each for you . . . Here . . . (*He hands four out, pockets the remainder.*) Don't start boozing after your turn. I've promised the Principal we'll be out by ten at the latest. All set then. Let's get to the van . . .

(*They troop out one after the other,* WATERS *standing in the doorway to see them through. He gives a final cursory look around the room as he packs his briefcase and grabs his coat and hat. Sees* CONNOR'S *donkey jacket on the pipes, collects it, leaves. Sounds of footsteps, muffled talking. After a moment, car and van doors being opened and closed, engines starting up. The door opens and the* CARETAKER *peeps in, sees the room vacated, advances. He carries a smashed chair, the frame in the right hand, a leg in the left. After a moment, he sights* PATEL'S *muslin-covered package. Stops, scans. Signs of slight but rising apprehension. He reaches gingerly towards it with the chair leg. Touches. Prods more vigorously, yet still cringing from it, as though half expecting an explosion. Nothing. He drops the chair leg, opens the neck of the bag, peers in, sniffs, sniffs again, sniffs several times, his face crinkling with disgust. Stands. Picks up chair. Leaves, switching off all lights behind him.*)

ACT TWO

*A small club stage. A club pianist has arrived during
the interval and is just completing a medley of old
favourites. The* CONCERT SECRETARY *arrives at his
table at the side of the stage, calling "Yes, yes
all right Teddy. I'll see to it after the draw" to
someone Off Stage and at the same time showing*
CHALLENOR *(Scotch in hand) to his own table
Stage Right.*

SECRETARY. (*Dry, tolerably sour, in charge; but
real, not caricature.*) Right. As announced in last
week's club bulletin, there will now be a brief interval
in the bingo . . . (*Groans, calls of "No" etc.*) a *brief*
interval in the bingo, to listen to some new comics setting their feet on the first rung of the ladder of fame.
Now this'll last half an hour at the most and I'd like
you to show these lads the traditional courtesy of the
club . . . and then we'll get straight back to the bingo
as soon as it's all over. Now . . . these are all lads
who've been coached by that favourite comic of
yesteryear, the Lancashire Lad himself, Mr. Eddie
Waters. Take a bow, Eddie. (WATERS *appears and
makes his way to an empty table on the other side
of the stage, ignoring the* CONCERT SECRETARY'S *urgings
to say a few words, and sits down with his pint Stage
Left.*) So I think we're in for a treat. (*Checking tatty
notes.*) First off then, a young man from Ireland, now
domiciled in Moss Side, your welcome please for . . .
Mick . . . Connor. (CONNOR *appears from the wings
in hired evening dress and black pumps, a white*

42

*Carnation and black dickie. Pianist covers his entrance
with "If you're Irish, come into the parlour.")*

CONNOR. (*Very Irish.*) I told him not to say any-
thin' about me bein' Irish. I wanted to creep up on yez
like. (*The* CONCERT SECRETARY *shushes the audience
authoritatively.* CONNOR *angles his head in the* CON-
CERT SECRETARY'S *direction.*) I'm talkin' as quiet as I
can. (*To audience.*) Good evening. Sorry about de
bingo. (*Takes microphone from stand, begins a slow,
easy walk that will take him down from the club stage
and find him sitting on the theatre stage below.*) Wuz
yez ever foreigners, any of yez? I don't mean the odd
fortnight in Brighton now, I mean like always. Jeez,
it's a funny thing . . . First day in Manchester I go
lookin' for rooms. Your woman answers the door, a
neat little thing wi' gouty eyes, I says "Do you have
any low terms for Irishmen here?", she says "Yes. Piss
off." Mind you that was before the blacks came to
help us out, shoulder some of the white man's burden.
Troublemakers. I never knew we wuz troublemakers
till I got to England. You don't you know. I mean,
what are you lot, eh, do you know? You don't have
to find out, do you? Just people. You'd have to go to
India or . . . Africa . . . or Ireland to find out.
Mmm? They'd tell yer right enough. Well, stick
around, maybe we'll come to you. You know, even the
Catholic Church is different here. I went to Mass at
the Holy Name, like a bloody opera. Back home in
Wexford it's more like a market. The priest charges
ten percent commission on all transactions. And con-
fessions . . . Jesus . . . in England you can hear the
candles melt, so you can . . . Your Irish priest is
either half deaf or half stewed, "Speak up my son,
there's nothing to be ashamed of . . ." so you've
gotta burst your lungs off to get absolution, safact.

(*Bellow.*) Bless me Father for I have sinned, it is six years since my last confession . . . I have missed Mass seven hundred and twenty three times . . . I have fornicated . . . (*Own voice.*) *Then* you can hear a pin drop. I tell yer, we'd sit there by the confession box every Saturday night . . . all the young buckos . . . it was a great way for picking up girls for the dance. (*Acting it.*) Hey, dissun puts out . . . ten times widat Heaney feller from Ballamadurphy . . . Hey, wait while you hear where he put his finger . . . (*He laughs.*) None of that here, mind. Your English priest enjoys it too much . . . Oh yes. (*English priest's voice, dripping with retracted interest, low and breathy, close to microphone.*) Yes, I see, my son, and *you* put your hand where? (*Self, very low, hesitant but intense.*) I put it . . . down, her mouth, Father. (*Priest, slight but controlled increase in excitement.*) Did you now? Erm . . . and why did you do that, my son? (*Self.*) She 'ad dis . . . bone stuck, Father . . . (*Own voice.*) Or there's the other sort, the feller that's gonna end up Bishop's secretary, he's very bored . . . (*Bored posh priest, testy.*) All right, so you've been wearing your sister's clothes *again,* don't you ever do anything else? . . . Don't you fancy your mother's . . . I mean, you're in here every week with the same story, there's no plot, there's no development, look, it might excite you, there's absolutely nothing in it for me. Your penance is five Our Fathers and five Hail Marys . . . and the next time you're tempted to get into a frock just . . . count to ten . . . and ask God to make you a little more inventive. (*Pause.*) Reminds me of the old spinster lady back home confesses fornication and the priest asks her for details . . . 'cause he's interested like . . . and so he can get a good sight of her through the grille, so she tells him about this wonderful night of love she spent with a tinker, and the priest says, Mary McGuire, thats the most shameful thing you're after telling me and you a respected spinster of seventy three. And she says (*Old maid's girlish voice.*) as a matter of fact, Father, I was thirty when it happened, I just like talking about it. (*Pause.*) I married an English Catholic girl you know. She's sitting on the bed, on our honeymoon, and I see her take out these little yellow, tablety things, I says what's that, she says the pill, why, can't you take it in Ireland, and I says oh, I can take it all right, it's the women that aren't allowed. I says, How come you're on the pill? She says: Our church says we must search our own individual consciences for the truth and then act accordingly. (*Self.*) Did you ever hear of such a thing? Back home in Ireland them's what we call Protestants. 'Course we had other ways. Oh yes, we were very inventive. An uncle of mine practiced coitus interruptus all his life . . . till he got it right. I had lots of cousins in Wexford . . . God . . . (*Long reflective pause.*) he was a sad man, though. So listen anyway. Don't believe all you hear, you know what I mean. Speak well of the living. Especially within earshot. And the next time you meet an Irishman, count to ten . . . and ask God to make you a little bit more inventive. And don't keep slapping him on the back. One day he'll stick a pack of dynamite up his jacket and blow your bloody arm off. If he didn't do it already. Like the IRA man who knocks at the gates of Heaven and St. Peter says Who're you? And your man says "I'm from the IRA. and St. Peter says 'Oh no, you can't come in here' and your man says "I don't wanna come in, I'm giving yez all three minutes to get out." Goodnight. God bless.

(*Pianist plays through* CONNOR'S *applause and exit.*)

SECRETARY. (*Microphone.*) A Manchester man now, from Middleton, a warm welcome please for . . . (*Reading.*) . . . Mr. Sammy Samuels. (SAMMY *walks on. He wears a fine-fitting white jacket, red carnation, black bow, red satin handkerchief, diamond cufflinks.*)

SAMUELS. A message for any nymphomaniacs in the audience . . . Hello. Sit down, lady, we'll have no rushing the stage. 1929 I were born. Year of the Great Crash. The sound of me father's jaw dropping. He took one look at me and said, "I'm not that Jewish. Nobody's that Jewish." So, anyway, in the divorce court the judge awards me mother twenty pounds a month maintenance. And me father says: Judge, dat's very generous of you and to tell you de truth, ven business gets better I'll mebbe also help out a little. Anyway, me mother's bringing us all up like and me sister comes home from college and she says I'm afraid I can't continue with me studies, momma. Vy? says momma. She couldn't say why. Vy. Always vy. Vy, she says. My sister says I'm sort of . . . pregnant, momma. That did it . . . a chair, a seltzer, oi, oi . . . finally she says, So who's de fadder? My sister says momma, it's difficult to . . . pinpoint the father. . . . You don't know de fadder? I send you to college, I'm simple people, You got education, I don't know de proper vay to be introduced but you don't even know to ask Mit whom am I having de pleasure?! Something's running down my leg; I hope it's sweat. She was some woman, momma. Bank manager rings up, he says Mrs. Samuels, you have an overdraft of 50 pounds. Is dat so? she says. So vot vos de balance last month? He looks, he says: You had a credit of 22 pounds. All right, says momma, and did I call you?

(*He looks at the stone-faced* CHALLENOR, *wipes his hands on the handkerchief.*) O.K., forget the Jews. Everybody else did. Here, there was this poacher, see. Poacher? And he catches this deer. And he slings it over his shoulder and he's humping it through the forest and a gamekeeper catches him and he says, Hey you, you're poaching. And the guy says, How do mean? And the gamekeeper says, You've got a deer on your back. And the guy goes . . . (*Looks over his shoulder and screams.*) Heard about the Irish lamppost? Pissed on a dog. Hear about the Irish cargo ship carrying yoyos? Sank 44 times. The Irish waterpolo team. Drowned 12 horses. This secretary runs into the boss's office and says, "Can I use your dictaphone?" He says, "No, use your fingers like everyone else!" There's this West Indian tries to get a labouring job on a building site. Foreman says, No chance, I know you lot. I give one of you a job, you turn up the next day with a gang of your friends. He begs and pleads and finally he gets the job. Next day he turns up with a pigmy. (*Indicating.*) Pigmy. Down there. The foreman said, What did I tell you, no friends! He says, Thats not my friend, that's my lunch. What do you think of this Women's Lib, then? Burnt your bras have you? Did you, sir, how interesting. I burnt the wife's. She went bloody mad, she was still in it. I'm in a pub downtown and this liberated woman person collars me, she says, You're a brutal, loudmouthed, sadistic, irrational, sexist, male chauvinist pig. I said, I suppose a quick screw is out of the question . . . So later in bed, I'm giving her one and she says, You're marvellous, you're marvellous. No one has ever made love to me like that before. But, I'm sort of kinky. Would you mind biting my ears while you're doing it? Sure. On the lobes, gentle like. (*He mimes the delicate*

lobe bites, quite slowly.) Now, she says, can you kiss
my bust real quick? (*He repeats lobes slowly, then
adds the rapid bust kisses.*) Now, she says, can you
put your hands round the back here and pull on the
cheeks . . . Certainly. (*He starts the mime at the top,
adding the buttock-tugging, returns to the lobes
again.*) She says "You've slipped out!" I said "No
bloody wonder, I've forgotten what I was doing!" I
was at the bar there earlier and I thought I'd take a
leak while it was slack. A big black bugger rushes in.
Aaaah, he says. Just made it! I took a look, I said,
There's no chance of making one in white for me is
there? I'd like to thank the pianist. (*Fast.*) Thanks.
Actually he's a brilliant pianist, this man. He has
a lovely touch. Actually, he got that touch off Liberace.
(*To pianist.*) Am I right? And that other thing you
got off Liberace . . . has it cleared up? O.K., take
care of yourselves, and if any of you ladies are accosted
on your way out by a dark, handsome young fellow
in a white jacket and a red carnation, just remember,
it's for your own good. I leave you with this thought:
impotence is just nature's way of saying Forget it.
But remember . . . Maestro (*To pianist. Sings, When
You're Smiling. Bows, takes, applause, leaves with
mike, returns mike to* CONCERT SECRETARY, *exits.*)

SECRETARY. (*Slowly returning microphone to stand.*)
Two lads now from Blackley . . . a double act . . .
Phil and Ged Murray . . . who call themselves . . .
(*Checking scrap of paper, nose wrinkling.*) . . .
Night and Day.

(*Pianist plays 'Night and Day' to cover the entrance.*
PHIL MURRAY, *in black dinner jacket and bow
tie, pulls on a huge whicker basket, gestures to
the deeply reluctant* CONCERT SECRETARY *to help*

*him lift it onto the club stage. When he's got it
set, he takes from it a small girl dummy, shy,
long blond hair, party dress.*)

PHIL. (*A good "best" voice.*) Good evening ladies
and gentlemen. Say good evening, Sophie.

DOLL. (*Eyelashes demure.*) Good evening.

PHIL. Are you ready to sing your song then, Sophie?

GED. (*Strangulated, from box: minimal but effective
dummy voice.*) Hey.

PHIL. (*Ignoring him.*) What's it going to be then,
Sophie?

GED. (*Louder.*) Hey. I'm talking to you.

PHIL. (*Side of mouth.*) Shut up. Sophie?

GED. Listen, I'm not lying here all bloody night.
Have you got that stupid stick-doll in 'ere?

PHIL. Be quiet.

GED. Y'ave, 'avn't you? Y'ave. You mighta lain 'im
down.

PHIL. Excuse me, Sophie . . . (*He opens the trunk,
places the doll on* GED'S *stomach, closes it again.*)
Ladies and gentlemen, we *were* going to start with a
song . . .

GED. (*To the girl doll in the trunk, voice warm and
sexy.*) Hello, love. (*Carries on flirting and laughing—
as though being tickled.*) Hey, what you doing down
there, hey, what you doing . . . (*Etc.*)

(PHIL *abandons his attempts to entertain the audience,
begins to get* GED *out of the trunk. It's a painful
floppy process. They flounder to the tall stool by
the microphone. Their patter throughout is serious, desperate.*)

PHIL. (*Fixing him on his thigh.*) Right, now sit
there and sit still. (GED'S *dressed and made up as a*

ventriloquist's dummy, in Manchester city supporter's colours, sky blue and white scarf, woollen hat, rattle, rosette. His blue and white half football boots are tied to his ankles, i.e. not on his feet. He slips off PHIL'S *knee, is dragged back, all in one movement. Perches finally.*) Can't you stay up?

GED. Longer than you can, if your wife's to be believed.

PHIL. That's enough.

GED. (*From side of mouth.*) Face front and keep smiling. *Smile,* you fool. They might go away.

PHIL. Where have you been then?

GED. Evening. Nice out, sir, I might get mine out in a minute. (*To* PHIL.) That didn't go over too well. You were moving your lips, you dummy.

PHIL. I said, where have you been?

GED. (*Deliberately posh.*) Where have I been? Where have I been? I've been to the football match, haven't I, you daft pillock, where do you think I've been? Manchester City. (*Waves rattle, own voice.*) My dad were a Manchester City fan. (*Rattle.*) My dad said if he came home and found one of the city football team in bed with the old lady he'd brew him a cup of tea. (*The joke dies.* GED *waits for* PHIL *to throw the next line at him.*) He said, if he came home and found one of the team in bed with me mother he'd brew him a cup of tea . . .

PHIL. (*Suddenly diverging from the act; no warning.*) Look, if you're so funny, why don't you tell us all a joke?

GED. (*Turning his head to look at his brother and blinking a question.*) What?

PHIL. (*Uneasy at once, but insistent.*) Tell us the one about the Pakistani up on a rape charge.

GED. (*Half out of the act, trying to think, looking in*

WATERS' *direction, as if for help.*) What you talking about?

PHIL. (*Faintly desperate.*) Tell the joke. (GED *turns his head slowly, stares at the audience, stands, very slowly, puts his hands on his brother's shoulders, removes him from the stool, takes his place, draws his brother carefully down onto his thigh, repositions the microphone stand.*)

GED. (*In character.*) *You* tell it. (PHIL *blinks, thinks.*)

PHIL. (*Terrified, struggling for confidence.*) There's this Pakistani, see, up on a rape charge. So the coppers decide they'll have an identity parade. And they get eight or nine other Pakkies and they put this one at the front and explain what they're doing. Then they bring in the girl and the Pakistani shouts. (*Pakistani voice.*) She is the one, Officer. No doubt about it . . . (GED *and* PHIL *stare whitely out at the audience. Neither knows where to go next.* GED *gets up, repeats the procedure in reverse until he's back on* PHIL'S *knee.*)

GED. (*Finally.*) How about that song?

PHIL. Why not?

GED. A song entitled If I had it all to do over again, I'd do it all over you. How'd you like being the dummy?

PHIL. (*A nightmare: wholly dependent on his brother now.*) Not a lot.

GED. No. It's not funny, is it?

PHIL. How d'you mean?

GED. Shall I tell you some'at. There's two fellers like and they're both crippled. One hasn't moved his hands for twenty years and the other's in a wheelchair paralyzed from the neck down. And they go to Lourdes for a miracle cure. And they get to Lourdes and the priest calls for the one with the hands and he goes down and the priest immerses his hands in the water and he says In nomine domine homminie wommine like they do you know and suddenly the feeling comes back to his hands and he can use them again. He says, it's a miracle. For twenty years I haven't been able to use my hands and he helps to push his dear old friend in the wheelchair into the water up to his neck and the priest says In nomine homine womine and they pull him out and there's four new tyres on the chair.

PHIL. Maybe we should sing the song?

GED. Have a look at your watch. (PHIL *looks*.) What's it say?

PHIL. Time for a song.

GED. (*Back in the act's groove at last.*) I'm not going back in that box after.

PHIL. Sing the song.

GED. All right, but I'm warning you, you *walk* me off, sod your hernia, I'm not going in there with her and that cricket stump . . .

PHIL. Maestro, please.

HE'S MY BROTHER
OUR KID
DON'T WANT ANOTHER
OUR KID
HE WATCHES OVER ME
WHEN THINGS GET TOUGH
HE PULLS THE STRINGS
THAT WIPE THE TEARS AWAY ON MY
    CUFF
HE'S MY BROTHER
OUR KID
AND THERE'S NO OTHER
OUR KID

HE IS MY FRIEND, MY MATE AND MY
    MUCKER
HE IS MY BROTHER
OUR KID.

*(They take bows like automations, GED striding off
first, PHIL following whitely, lugging the basket.
Pianist covers.)*

SECRETARY. Another Irishman now (GED *and* PHIL
explode into violent recriminations in the wings. The
CONCERT SECRETARY *looks frowningly behind* him.)
—from Belfast this one—good job we kept 'em apart—
hands together please for . . . George . . . McBrain.

*(*MCBRAIN *on, carrying a hand-microphone. The
mania glands sweating freely. He wears a fine
maroon evening jacket, horn-rimmed glasses on
nose end, frills at chest and cuffs of royal blue
shirt.)*

MCBRAIN.
In the garden of Eden lay Adam
Complacently stroking his madam
And long was his mirth
For he knew that on earth
There were only two ***—and he had 'em.
I had a hundred jokes standing back there, I can't
remember a one of 'em. (*He looks at the audience:
stares.*) Never mind, I'm good to look at. There's this
coloured feller on his way to work. (*Stops.*) Don't
you think that's funny? There's this very honest Jew.
No favourites here. There's this very brilliant Irish-
man. From Dublin. I tried to get the wife to come.
It gets harder, I dunnit though. I don't say she's

jealous but she's the only woman I know. If music
be the food of love, how about a bite of your maracas?
I was in bed with the wife last Thursday. The wife lay
there, very quiet, smoking her pipe. I leaned across
and I said do you fancy anything, Heart? And she
said: Yes, I fancy an African about six-foot-three
with a big fat . . . cheque book. (*To audience.*) Don't
get ahead of yourselves! Naughty! I said: Yeah? And
what do you reckon he'd make of that great fat idle
bum of yours? And she said: What makes you think
we'd be talking about you? Doesn't say a lot, my
wife. Talks all the time but doesn't say a lot. I took
her to the zoo. Belle Vue, to see the orang-utan.
Enormous. Great painted whatsits, like rump-steak.
(*Bunching hands, stomps a bit, pulls the face.*) Like
Idi Amin having a shower. She falls right over the
wire, as sure as I'm standing here, she trips clean over
the wire and lands on her back with her legs parted,
her skirt up and her drawers flapping in the wind.
I couldn't look, it was horrible. The big feller kinda
sniffs and ambles towards her, and . . . he ends up
poised above her, like that, and the wife whispers
(*Breathless terror.*) George, what shall I do? What
shall I do? And I said (*Whisper.*) Tell HIM you've
got a headache . . . Had a look at the alligators.
Just floating handbags really. She's been a goer in her
time, I tell you. Fast? I met her at a dance in Belfast,
I said: Excuse me. She grabbed me by the lapels and
stuck her tongue half-way down me throat. I was
only asking for a light. We had a whirlwind romance,
I wined her and dined her every week for a fortnight,
bean soup, pie and peas, whirlwind. Then I plucked
up courage enough to say the words I never imagined
myself saying in a million years: You're WHAT? And
she was. God, what a slut. I went to see her father

. . . out to the Maze prison . . . him and his six lads all in there together . . . I never saw a family like it. Ugly? Listen they wore hoods before they joined the terrorists, safact. The neighbours made 'em, protect the kids. First thing he says, You're not a mick, are you? Certainly not, says I. So why didn't you use something, says he. Use something? says I. Listen, the first time I met your daughter she was wearing a notice pinned to her chest saying I am an epileptic and will die unless you lie on top of me, there wasn't time for anything like that . . . Seamus, big friend of mine from Cork (*Ape gestures.*) . . . Oh no, that's the monkey . . . (*Straightens into Franken-stein.*) Seamus, not very bright . . . He got a pair of water-skis for Xmas, spent the next three months looking for a sloping lake. True. Joined the IRA. Tried to blow up the Queen Elizabeth. Couldn't get his mouth around the funnel. But see my wife, God she's a slut though. Every time I go for a leak the sink is full of dishes. And the food, instant pollution. She gave us rabbit for a fortnight once, every meal. Rabbit pie, rabbit stew, rabbit rashers, rabbit pâté, rabbit trotters . . . rabbit eggs . . . After two weeks I was done in, I collapsed holding my stomach. She said: I'll send for the doctor. I said: Sod the doctor, see if you can borrow a ferret. But . . . Let's face it, few of us are perfect. Not even the Irish. I was in Belfast the other week, there's a feller lying out on the pavement with a bullet hole in his forehead. There's an old lady walks by, she stops and looks down at yer man for a minute, then she crosses herself and she says: Well, thank God it missed his eye. You can't hate 'em can you. Listen, I've gotta go, I'm wife swapping tonight. I gorra bloke's greyhound last week, made a change. So listen, I'll see yer, all right? (*He*

*takes his bow, sweating, a bit concerned, stiff with
tension now, not looking in* WATERS *direction.* MCBRAIN
catches WATERS' *eye, in a bow: a still moment.* MC-
BRAIN *breaks, disappears.*)

SECRETARY. (*Microphone.*) Last, this evening, a
young man from Clayton making his first appearance
before an audience, I'm told . . . a warm hand for
. . . Gethin Price.

(PRICE *emerges, carrying the tiny violin and bow.
He wears bagging half mast trousers, large sullen
boots, a red hard wool jersey, studded and bat-
tered denim jacket, sleeves rolled to elbows, a red
and white scarf tied onto an arm. His face has
been subtly whitened, to deaden and mask the
face. He is half clown, half this year's version of
bovver boy. The effect is calculatedly eerie, funny
and chill. He takes out a deeply filthy handkerchief, spreads it carefully, expertly across his right
shoulder, slowly tucks the tiny violin on his left,
stands perfectly still, looks for the first time at
the audience. Cocks the bow, stares at it intently,
apparently sinking into process. Notices a very
fine thread of gut hanging down. Shakes the bow.
Shakes it again. The thread hangs on. He brings
the bow finally to his mouth, tries to bite the
thread off, his teeth are set on edge, he winces
mutely, tries again, can't. He thinks. Tries, bend-
ing oddly on one leg, to trap the thread under his
huge boot. Fails. Thinks. Takes out a lighter. Sets
fire to the thread. Satisfaction. Makes as if to
play. The cocked bow slowly begins to smoulder
at the far end. He waves it about, horrified. The
violin now begins to play unaided in his other
hand a piece of intricate Bach. He's trapped for*

a moment between the two events; finally he places the spent bow on the stage, puts the violin under his boot, dimps it like a cigarette until it's thoroughly crushed.)

PRICE. (*To himself, not admitting the audience's existence.*) Wish I had a car. I feel like smashing a car up. Smashing the headlamps. Slashing the tires. Stealing the hub caps. On me own. I feel really strong. Wish I had a car. I could do with some exercise. (*He does a complicated kata, with preying mantis foot-sweeps, a tan-tui, pa-kua dao, and other Kung Fu exercises. A spot suddenly illuminates larger than life-size dummies of a youngish man and woman (Carried on by a club-hand.): well dressed, beautiful people, a faint, unselfconscious arrogance in their carriage. The man wears evening dress, gloves, etc., the girl, a simple, stunning white full-length dress and wrap. Her arm is looped in his. They stand, perhaps waiting for a cab to show after the theatre. He has continued his exercises throughout this "arrival." Becomes aware of them gradually: rises slowly: stares. Turns to the audience, slowly smiles, evil and childlike. Sniffs. Ambles over. Stands by the man, measuring, walks round to stand by the girl. We sense him being ignored. He begins to inspect the girl minutely. Takes a cigarette from pocket.*) Cigarette? (*Nothing. He offers it to the man.*) No? (*He pockets the cigarette, turns, calls.*) "Taxi!" (*Sharply, out front, shakes his head as it disappears. Moves round to the man's side again.*) Are you the interpreter then? Been to the football match, have we? Were you at t'top end wi' lads? Good, wannit? D'you see Macari? Eh? Eh? See him moving that ball around? Eh? (*Silence.*) P'raps I'm not here. Don't you like me? You hardly know me. Let's go

and have a pint, get to know each other. Here, don't
you live in Salford? I swear I've seen you at the race
track. (*Nothing. He takes a cigarette out of the man's
top pocket.*) Very kind of you. Ta. (*He lights the
cigarette, blows the smoke in slow separate puffs
across the man's face.*) Int this nice? I like a good
chat. (*Intimate, man-to-man.*) Eh. I bet she puts out,
dunt she, sunshine? She's got a fair pair of knockers
on her too. Has she been around? Does she ever go
dancing at the Lyceum Satdays? I think Eric Yates
took her home one night. If it's her, she's a right goer,
according to Eric. (*Pause.*) I don't know whether to
thump you or what. I suppose I could just give you a
clout, just to let you know I exist. (*He blows smoke
into the man's face.*) Is that hair dyed? Looks dyed.
Are you a puff? Are you a pufter? (*Sniffs. Front, fast.*)
Taxi! (*Pause.*) That's not a taxi, it's a hearse. (*Evilish
grin.*) You're getting confused, lady. Unless you were
thinking of getting a quick fun funeral in before re-
tiring for the night. (*To man.*) Say something, Alice?
She's calling hearses, he's talking to himself. (*He turns
back to the man.*) You do *speak*, do you? I'm trying
to *talk* to you. Say some'at. Tell us what kind of day
you've had. Are you on the buses? Eh. Shall I make
you laugh? This feller pays twenty pounds for this
whore, right? Only she dunt fancy him and runs out
of the room. He chases her, stark nekkid, down t'
street. Cop stops him, says Where's the fire, lad?
Feller says, I've no idea, but if you see a nude bird
running down street, *fuck* her, it's paid for. (*Pause.
Nothing.*) You can laugh, you know, I don't mind you
laughing. I'm *talking* to you . . . There's people'd call
this *envy*, you know, it's not, it's hate. (*Now very
fast.*) Are you bi-sexual or is that your sister? You'll
never get a taxi here, they're all up at Piccadilly wait-

ing for t' last train from London. Ask me how I know. I work there that's why. And don't interrupt when I'm talking, dint your mother ever tell you, it's rude? (*He does a King Fu thrust, missing the man's head by inches.*) Bruce Lee, do you like him? God, he is. You're a stuck-up bastard, aren't you? Aren't you? Aren't you? Puff. Pufter. (PRICE *halts his burble. Blinks. Pads round to stand at woman's side.*) Say something? (*In her ear.*) Listen . . . I've got a British Rail delivery truck round the corner, ditch Alice and we'll do the town. (*He notices a folded copy of the Times in the man's hand. Passes behind the figures, pops his head between them.*) Crosswords? (*Thinks a moment.*) Election. Nine across. Big poll in China question mark. (*Chinaman.*) E-lection. (PRICE *looks from one to the other, laughs suddenly. He takes hold of their handles, begins to lift them up and down, to indicate their mirth.*) Election! Election! Big poll in China. Laugh you buggers, laugh! (PRICE *exhorts them to laugh, squeezing their bodies up and down and voicing their laughter for them. Then very suddenly.*) Here. (*He takes a flower out of his pocket, offers it to them.*) For the lady. No, no, I have a pin. (*Pause. He pins the flower—a marigold—with the greatest delicacy between the girl's breasts. Steps back to look at his work.*) No need for thanks. My pleasure entirely. Believe me. (*Silence. Nothing. Then a dark red stain, gradually widening, begins to form behind the flower.*) Aagh, aagh, aagh, aagh . . . (*The spot shrinks slowly on the dummies, centering finally on the red stain.* PRICE's *"Aaghs" become short barks of laughter. Innocence.*) I wonder what happened. P'raps it pierced a vein. (*Their light goes altogether. We're left with his single, chill image.*) I made them laugh, though. (*Depressed.*) Who needs *them?* Hunh.

Who needs them? We manage. (*Chanting.*) Un-i-ted. Uni-ted. You won't keep us down there for long, don't worry. We're coming up *there* where we can gerrat yer. (*Chants.*) Lou Macari, Lou Macari . . . I shoulda smashed him. They allus mek you feel sorry for 'em, out in the open. I suppose I shoulda just kicked him without looking at him. (*Pause. He looks after them. Calling.*) National Unity? Best joke I've heard all night. (*Pause. He picks up the tiny violin, i.e. another, switched, uncrushed, and a bow. Sings the first two lines of The Red Flag then plays them, simple and direct.*) Still, I made the buggers laugh . . . (*He walks off. The* CONCERT SECRETARY *probably shocked, embarrassed, not wishing to dwell. Lights fade.* WATERS *stands, face gaunt, grey.* CHALLENOR *tosses down a scotch, sheafs his notes, pockets pen.*)

SECRETARY. That's the lot, ladies and gentlemen. You have your cards, I think. Charlie Shaw has 'em for them that hasn't, and we're starting right away, settle yourselves down now. And it's eyes down for a full house . . . (*Lights fade gradually.*) Always look after . . . Number One. (*Lights fade to black.*)

END OF ACT TWO

ACT THREE

Classroom. Time: 9:43. Empty. Rain beats on win-
dows. McBRAIN, SAMUELS *and* CONNOR *return*
slowly, to sit in their respective places, though
an almost deliberate distance apart. PHIL MUR-
RAY *in. They sit, glum, drained, separate.*

Simple exhaustion underpins the low, tense, anxious,
angry, baffled mood of the four. No eye contacts.
People sit or fiddle. SAMUELS *sits in his coat,*
ready for away. CONNOR *is again pretty wet.*
McBRAIN *has changed back to his parka and*
jeans, his bag on the desk in front of him.

PRICE, *off, suddenly starts up with "There's No Busi-*
ness Like Show Business . . ."

PHIL. Listen to that stupid cunt.
SAMUELS. There'll be no pigging business for *him*,
that's for a certainty. Did you ever see anything like
it? He's bloody bananas.

(PRICE *in, dressed as in act one: smells the mood of*
the others; dwells for a moment in the doorway.)

McBRAIN. (*Bleak.*) Did you see that Challenor
feller? He smiled twice all evening, and both times
it was at some'at the sodding concert secretary said.
CONNOR. (*Low.*) I don't reckon it was much fun for
Mr. Waters either.

61

PHIL. (*Checking door with a look.*) Look, sod Mr. Waters. He's not handing jobs out, is he, Seamus.

CONNOR. (*Dangerous, suddenly, very deliberate.*) My name's Mick. (*Silence.*)

McBRAIN. Take it easy, Michael . . .

CONNOR. (*Ignoring him.*) Mick.

PHIL. All right. Mick.

(GED MURRAY *has appeared wet through in the doorway, in time for the last exchange.*)

GED. (*Finally.*) Fish and chips. It's teeming down out there.

McBRAIN. About bloody time. Did you nip home to make 'em?

GED. Ha bloody ha. There was a queue a mile bloody long. It's next to t' Roxy Cinema, innit. (*He's with* SAMUELS.) They dint have any halibut. I got you a pie.

SAMUELS. A pie? What d'you get a pie for?

GED. (*Handing it to him.*) I thought you might be hungry.

SAMUELS. (*Opening package.*) A pie? I don't eat pies.

GED. (*To* PRICE, *giving him packet.*) Hey, that was great, Geth. (PRICE *winks.* GED *throws* PHIL's *packet of chips at his brother, walks heavily off down the room, passing his own desk and fetching up at* PRICE's *where he sits, rather morose.*)

McBRAIN. They're stone bloody cold.

GED. It's a long bloody way.

SAMUELS. (*Staring at pie he's broken.*) It's a bloody *pork* pie!

GED. Is it? Don't you like pork?

SAMUELS. God Almighty, I ask for a piece of fish, he brings me a pork pie!

PRICE. Holy pig! Here, give it us here! (*Takes pie, carries it over to the desks, notes his own taken, stands finally behind* GED'S *chair, leans on chairback very deliberately, regards the other five very carefully for a moment without speaking. Then, in sermon voice:*) Dearly beloved, we are gathered here in the sight of Mammon to mourn the passing of several very promising careers in the comedic arts. For those who live on . . . the words of the great and holy musical "The Song of Norway" will be of special comfort: De cuntibus minibus tuum, rectum anus mirabilis est. Which loosely translated means: It's easy to be a bit of a cunt, you've got to work at becoming a shithouse. Here endeth lesson one. (*He blesses them gravely, sits down. Silence.*)

SAMUELS. (*Finally, ugly.*) You got anyone . . . special in mind, Charlie?

PRICE. (*He gets up swiftly, crosses to the dais, picks up a chair leg left by the* CARETAKER, *holds it in two hands a foot or so from his forehead, breathes very deeply three or four times, then smashes it cleanly with his forehead. He carries the two ends to* SAMUELS, *puts them carefully on his desk.*) You wanna crucify the man, you do the job properly, Sammy. (*He turns, walks away, resumes his seat.* SAMUELS *grasps the two ends,* MCBRAIN *takes them from him with gentle power, carries them to the waste paper basket.*)

MCBRAIN. There was this feller, see . . .

CONNOR. (*Fraying.*) No more jokes, George. All right? (MCBRAIN *deposits the ends, returns to his seat. Silence.* GED *finishes his chips, wipes his hands on the paper.*)

GED. (*Casual, innocent, knowing.*) You'll be allright, George. You knew what to do all right.

McBRAIN. (*Serious, tough, close to great anger.*) So when do I get the 30 pieces of silver? I don't want inquests. I want work.

SAMUELS. Right! Who the fuck does he (PRICE.) think he is anyway! (*To* PRICE.) What about your . . . performance then, Coco the bloody clown? It was bloody embarrassing . . .

GED. (*Generous, serious.*) It were different.

SAMUELS. Different? It was putrid. Different from bloody comedy, that's for sure.

CONNOR. Look, for Jesus Christ's sake, it's over, will you forget it . . .

GED. Hey, *you* were good, Mick, what I could hear of it. You got most of 'em in too, dint you.

CONNOR. Yeah. I went down like a fart at a funeral.

PHIL. What a bleeding audience. Thick as pig shit.

PRICE. (*Dangling a chip from finger and thumb.*) A bad lover blames his tool.

SAMUELS. So why didn't the great Lancashire Lad do a warm-up then, eh? He sent you out cold, and I had to follow you.

GED. Oh, *you* found your feet all right, Sammy . . .

SAMUELS. What does that mean then?

(*The* CARETAKER *comes in, a large battery lamp in his hand.*)

CARETAKER. You lot still here? I'm waiting to lock up you know. I've got a home to go to. Somebody left that thing . . . (*He points to the muslin sack. He leaves, turning to* WATERS.)

WATERS. We won't be long now . . .

CARETAKER. I hope not. I'm not on overtime you

know . . . (*He leaves.* WATERS *stands a moment in the doorway looking into the room. They stare, some of them, half-turning, at him. He's white, drained, tired and old. He walks, less spryly, to the desk. Sits down. Stares at the desk top. Silence. Some looks round the room.*)

GED. (*Holding them up.*) There's a packet of chips if you want them, Mr. Waters. (WATERS *looks at him, makes no answer.* CHALLENOR *in, shaking his coat.*)

CHALLENOR. Sorry, gentlemen. Several calls of nature on the way. You won't have reached your prostates yet, but you will. Mind if I use the desk, Eddie? (WATERS *relinquishes the desk, goes to lean by the windows, an onlooker.* CHALLENOR *places his case down, opens it, removes notes and forms, flicks through them, sniffs. Looks at* PRICE *covertly once or twice. Gathers.*) Right, there's not much time so I'll get cracking. Interesting evening. Lot of promise. I'll take you one by one so we don't get mixed up. Mick Connor.

CONNOR. Yeah.

CHALLENOR. Yes. You've not done a lot, have you?

CONNOR. No, I've done nothing. Concerts, works do's.

CHALLENOR. I quite liked it. One or two quite nice jokes, quite nicely told. (*Studying notes.*) Bit old-fashioned, I thought, you know, following a single topic through your act. It mighta worked even so, if you'd taken something more up the audience's street. I mean, you might find being an Irishman in England fascinating, there's no reason we should, is there? (*Pause.*) Had a sort of . . . earnestness about it I didn't much take to. You know, as if you were giving a sermon. One thing you've gotta learn, people don't learn, they don't want to, and if they did, they won't look to the likes of us to teach 'em. You've got to be very good indeed to patronize your audience, I can tell you. (*Pause.*) The sex was crude. I've nothing against it, but it requires taste, if you see what I mean, I've never heard a good joke yet about coitus interruptus. Still, you had your moments. Some promise there. (*Turns* CONNOR'S *sheet onto its face.*) Sammy Samuels?

SAMUELS. Himself.

CHALLENOR. I thought you'd never get started. First thing you want to do is ditch the first half of your act.

SAMUELS. Yeah, it's stuff I've been shedding, you know . . .

CHALLENOR. S'too Jewish. What's a Jew nowadays, eh. Who wants to know I mean.

SAMUELS. Yeah, I can see that.

CHALLENOR. Same mistake as the Irishman. (*Looks at notes.*) Fortunately you pulled out of it and got very good. It was a different act, the wife, blacks, Irish, women, you spread it around, you can score, keep it tight they'll fall asleep on you. (*Pause.*) Liked the Women's Lib bits. (*Pause.*) You need an ending, you were just sticking one after another till you'd done. No climax. People want a climax.

SAMUELS. Yeah, I er . . . got off the rails a bit actually . . .

CHALLENOR. Stay on 'em. Phil and Ged Murray.

PHIL. Here.

CHALLENOR. Aye well, what went wrong there? (PHIL *and* GED *look at each other briefly.*) There was a distinct smell of cock-up on the air about halfway through. (*Reading notes.*) I've got a note about a Pakistani on a rape charge . . . Aye, that's it. What happened then? (PHIL *looks at* GED. *Finally.*)

GED. (*Very quietly.*) We got lost.

CHALLENOR. What was it, new material or something?

GED. Yeah. Something like that.

CHALLENOR. Well it was horrible. The cardinal sin for any performer is embarrassing the audience. *You* had 'em doing up their shoelaces and picking up old beer mats. (*Pause.*) I don't know. It's a nice idea, but you need the material, my God, if you're gonna carry it off.

GED. We missed a lot out, after we got lost.

CHALLENOR. (*Interest faded.*) I'm sure you did. I'm sure you did. Liked the song, nice sentiment. Quite catchy really . . . (*He slashes his pencil across their page of notes, turns over.*) George McBrain. (MCBRAIN *shows.*) Cracking opening. Bang. No messing. Liked it. Lot of sex but well handled, if you see what I mean. Near the knuckle but not half-way up the armpit. A question of taste. Knowing when to draw back. Even with yobboes like that lot down there. (*Pause.*) Quite subtle but not too subtle. "Tell *him* you've gotta headache . . ." "Floating handbags" . . . Yes, yes . . . Good character, I believed it, was all of a piece. Confident, a bit aggressive, like that. Like the joke about the thick Seamus. (*To* CONNOR.) See, that's what I mean, don't push your own particular prejudice, you're there on *their* terms, not your own. (*Notes again.*) Good ending. (*Nodding in* SAMUELS' *direction.*) See, it was *down*beat, but it was firm. You know, diminuendo.

SAMUELS. Yeah, I can see that . . .

CHALLENOR. (*There's a long pause now, as he stares at* PRICE'S *notes. People make sweating faces on their own chances.* WATERS *leans, half sits, against the window, staring nowhere, withdrawn, remote.* PRICE *has his head in the desk, comes out only when he hears his name.* (*Finally.*) Gethin Price. . . . (*Another pause. He looks across at* PRICE *finally, no nonsense, man to man* . . . PRICE *subtly imitates the no-nonsense air.* CHALLENOR *looks in* WATERS' *direction, seeking guidance.* WATERS *purses his lips, looks out of the window.*) Not a lot to say about your piece, Price. You have a certain talent maybe as a mime, something like that . . . What you did tonight just . . . won't do. Music hall maybe, but there *is* no music hall . . . You wanna be a comic, you'd better start somewhere else, there's no way you'll get started with what you've got. Not viable. You've got to speak to the audience, for God's sake. (*Pause. Studying notes.*) Personally, I found the content of your act . . . how shall I put it? . . . repulsive. (*He stares on at his notes.* PRICE *slowly resumes an upright position in the chair.*) And aggressively unfunny. (*He looks at* PRICE, *practisedly kindly.*) If you want to get on, lad, you'd better sort a few problems out first. Get some distance, see what I mean. Don't give us your hang-ups straight. Too hot too handle. (*Closes note-file decisively.*) Four golden rules. For all of you, though some more than others. One. All audiences are thick, collectively, but it's a bad comic who lets 'em know it. Two. Two laughs are better than one. Always. Three. You don't have to love the people, but the people *have* to love you. Four. Sell yourself. If you're giving it away, it won't be worth having. (*Pause.*) All right, I coulda left this till I got back south, but I'm not that sorta person. At the moment, on tonight, I'm interested in just two of you . . . you (MCBRAIN.) and you (SAMUELS.) . . . I've got forms here. ˙(*Holds them up.*) . . . enrolment. When these've been received, there'll be an agent to look after your business and develop your career. Don't give your jobs up just now, mind. There'll be time enough for that when you start getting the bookings.

(*He gives forms to* McBRAIN *and* SAMUELS.) For the rest of you, I'll see you again. Drop me a line, I'm approachable. Just as long as you've learnt your lessons from tonight, that is. It's not the talent's lacking; it's application of a few basic rules of professional life. (*Turns to* WATERS.) Thanks, Eddie. Nice evening. Some good lads. Few wild notions mebbe but . . . (WATERS *walks towards him, takes the proffered hand.*) I'm down at the Midland. How about a drink?

WATERS. Still full of shit, Bert. Fuller than a large intestine.

CHALLENOR. How's that, Eddie?

WATERS. You wouldn't know a comedian from a barrowload of crap.

CHALLENOR. (*Light, unruffled.*) Meaning you disagree. Oh. Send in a report.

WATERS. I don't belong, remember?

CHALLENOR. What do you expect? A hundred per cent?

WATERS. They were nobbled, Bert. They're great lads.

CHALLENOR. Your opinion. Don't be ungracious . . .

WATERS. Yeah. Enjoy the Midland.

CHALLENOR. (*Smiling evenly.*) Always do, Eddie. Like the best.

(CHALLENOR *picks up his briefcase, leaves with what dignity he can salvage. A deep, uneasy silence.* PRICE *tosses and catches the pork pie rhythmically, like a juggler.*)

PRICE. (*Without venom.*) There goes nothing. A man who doesn't rate Frank Randle, what does *he* know?

WATERS. (*Deliberately.*) He knows enough, Mr. Price. He knows where the door marked In is.

PRICE. Yeah, but you know where it leads? (*Looking at* McBRAIN *and* SAMUELS.) It leads to a room with a notice on the wall and the notice says "Kindly ensure that you leave this room as you found it." A shitheap.

McBRAIN. No need to be bitter, Geth. You'll make out . . . (PRICE *laughs, hard, unpleasant, remote.*)

PRICE. (*Perfect Ulster.*) Thanks, George. S'very good of you. Just you remember now . . . Stand you your ground. (McBRAIN *stands up, a little uncertainly. Picks up the bag.*)

McBRAIN. A comic's a comic's a comic. Ain't that right though. (*Sniff. Pause.*) Thanks, Mr. Waters. It's been a great great pleasure. I'll never forget what you've done for me . . .

WATERS. (*With effort.*) Yes. Enjoy yourself, George. I'll watch out for you.

McBRAIN. We'll have a drink sometime.

WATERS. Yes.

McBRAIN. Look after yourself. (*Turning.*) And you lot. Scrubbers. (*Going.*)

SAMUELS. (*Standing.*) Hang on, George. I'll give you a lift, we can stop off at the club for a drink.

McBRAIN. No good, Sammy. I'm late as it is. The wife's not bin too good lately . . . I'd best get off.

SAMUELS. She'll not begrudge you a celebration pint, surely to God?

McBRAIN. (*Steel suddenly.*) She begrudges me nothing, Sammy. (*Small silence. He leaves, kiln-fired, hard inside the compromise.*)

SAMUELS. How about you, Phil? (PHIL *shakes his head whitely.*) Well . . . Cheers, Mr. Waters. A pleasure to know you. (*Offers hand.*)

WATERS. (*Taking it.*) Aye.

SAMUELS. Hard work, by Christ. Lost me script completely tonight. Don't know how I kept going . . .

WATERS. No.

SAMUELS. Couldn'ta done it without you, Mr. Waters, that's for a certainty. (*He treks the lonely walk to the door. Leaves. Everyone stands, preparing to go.* PHIL MURRAY *suddenly stands, lifts his bag, slams it down on the desk.*)

PHIL. (*To* GED, *smouldering.*) You coming?

GED. (*Turning slowly.*) No. I'll catch a bus.

PHIL. It's pissing down.

GED. Yeah, well ... . I need the air.

PHIL. (*Vicious.*) Suit yourself. (*He turns to leave. Turns back again.*) Are you going up the Hospital Sunday, see Dad?

GED. Yeah. Why?

PHIL. (*Pulls a quid out of his back pocket, hands it to* GED.) Give him this will you? Some fags or some'at. Tell him I'll ... try and make it week after. (GED *takes the note.* PHIL *leaves.*)

CONNOR. (*Approaching* WATERS' *desk.*) Sorry if we let you down.

WATERS. Not you, son. Not in a million years. Stay that way, O.K.? (*He holds his hand out.* CONNOR *takes it.*) I'm ... sorry.

CONNOR. (*Soft.*) Get stuffed. (CONNOR *winks at* PRICE *and* GED MURRAY, *leaves briskly, stops suddenly in the doorway.*) Shit! I never told me copper joke! I've been working on it all week ... (*He bangs his temple with his palm several times.*) Dummy, dummy. (*He's gone.*)

GED. Anyone fancy a pint? I fancy a pint. Or seven. Better get me skates on. (*He crosses to* WATERS.) Will there be ... will you be doing this again another time, Mr. Waters?

WATERS. Yes, I've a few lads lined up starting May ...

GED. I'd like to come back, if you'd have me.

WATERS. No no. You need to *do* it now, Ged. You *have* it, lad.

GED. Mebbe, mebbe not. I wanna go solo see. (*Exchanges look with* PRICE.) That screw-up . . . it weren't nerves, it weren't . . . technique . . . it were deliberate. (*Pointing at door.*) Him. He wanted to put some'at in for Challenor. I wouldn't have it. (*Grins, sniffs.*) I thought it were going right well up to then. Felt good too.

WATERS. Remember the feeling. It's important. (*Hand out.*) Take care.

GED. (*Embarrassed.*) Oh, I nearly forgot. Erm. (*Small package from pocket.*) We . . . er . . . we clubbed together some of us and bought you this. (*He hands him the package, smiles, leaves. In the corridor, we hear the* CARETAKER *quizzing* GED.)

CARETAKER. (*Off.*) It's not a bloody all-night session is it? Because if it is I'm on the bloody phone to the Union right away . . . (WATERS *unwraps the package. It's a pipe.* WATERS *studies it.*)

PRICE. No one . . . clubbed together.

WATERS. (*Gravely.*) That's all right. I don't smoke a pipe either. (WATERS *begins to pack his things, put on his overcoat etc.* PRICE *watches him fascinated.*) I don't know what to say Gethin. It's late. Maybe you shouldn't ask. It's been a funny night all round. (*He waves towards the door. Pause.*) And you. You've always been a bit wild, it's why I liked you, reminded me of me at twenty-five. Tonight . . . (*He leaves it, fastens his bag.*) I don't know . . .

PRICE. Did you like what I did? I'm asking.

WATERS. Like? (*Pause.*) It was terrifying.

PRICE. You know what they did, don't you?

WATERS. Oh yes.

PRICE. Do you blame 'em?

WATERS. (*Emphatic.*) No. We make our own beds.

PRICE. (*Angry suddenly.*) I didn't sell you out, Eddie.

WATERS. (*He frowns, turns slowly, straightening, to face* PRICE.) Is that what you think I think?

PRICE. Samuels, McBrain, they're nothing. They'll float through the system like turds on the River Irwell, they sold out because they've nothing worth holding on to. You can't blame them for doing it any more than you can praise Connor and Ged Murray for not. They stayed put because they've nowhere else to go . . .

WATERS. Listen, don't go on, we'll talk again . . .

PRICE. I just wanted it to be *me* talking out there. I didn't want to do something *we'd* worked on. You know.

WATERS. (*Lifting very suddenly, disturbed.*) Look, I *saw* it, you don't have to tell me what I already know . . .

PRICE. I want you to see the *difference* . . .

WATERS. . . . I *see* the difference. God Almighty, I see it, I see it, I just . . . don't understand it.

PRICE. Well then why don't you listen to what I'm saying, Eddie? (*Silence.* WATERS *looks at the clock.*)

WATERS. All right. (*Pause.*)

PRICE. (*Quiet.*) I can't paint *your* pictures. (*Points to eyes.*) These see.

WATERS. It's not only what you see, it's what you feel when you see it . . .

PRICE. What *I* feel. *I* feel.

WATERS. No compassion, no truth. You threw it all out, Gethin. Love, care, concern, call it what you like, you junked it all over the side.

PRICE. I didn't junk it. It was never there . . .

WATERS. What're you talking about . . . ?

PRICE. . . . you're avoiding the question Eddie . . .

WATERS. What do you want me to say . . . ?

PRICE. . . . Was I good or was I crap . . . ?

WATERS. . . . You were *brilliant!* (*Pause.* PRICE *blinks.* WATERS *glowers at the new terrain.*)

PRICE. (*Slowly.*) But you . . . didn't like it. (WATERS *shakes his head. Soft, slow.*) Why not?

WATERS. Look, it's late, we'll talk another time . . .

PRICE. Why not, Eddie?

WATERS. All right. It had grace, control, timing, all the things we've worked on all these weeks . . . It wasn't human. It was drowning in hate. It was ugly. People aren't dummies. I don't care what class or what race or what religion or what sex, if you make people dummies, you've stopped being interested in their reality, in their truth . . .

PRICE. Truth? What do you know about the truth, Mr. Waters? You think the truth is beautiful? You knew it when you started off, Oldham Empire, the People's Music Hall, Colne Hippodrome, Bolton Grand, New Brighton Palace, Ardwick Empire, Ardwick Hippodrome, the Met, the Star in Ancoats . . . the Lancashire Lad—you knew it then all right. Nobody hit harder than Eddie Waters, that's what they used to say. Because you were still in touch with what made you . . . hunger . . . diptheria, filth, unemployment, penny clubs, means tests, bed bugs, head lice . . . Was all *that* truth beautiful? (*Pause.* WATERS *says nothing.*) Truth was a fist you hit with. Now it's like . . . now it's like cowflop, a day old, hard until it's underfoot and then it's . . . green, soft. Shitten. (*Pause.*) Nothing's changed, Mr. Waters, is what I'm saying. When I stand upright—like tonight at that club—I bang my head on the ceiling. Just like you fifty years ago. We're still caged, exploited, prodded and pulled at, milked, fattened, slaughtered, cut up, fed out. We still don't belong to ourselves. Nothing's changed. You've just forgotten, that's all. (WATERS *gathers his*

things about him, using the process.) And you . . .
stopped laughing, didn't you? Not even a warm-up
down at that club tonight. You had nothing to say to
those people down there, did you? (WATERS *turns
slowly to face him.*) In three months or more, you
never said a single funny thing. (*Pause.*) Challenor
reckons you could have been great . . . he said you
just stopped wanting it. Maybe you lost your hate,
Mr. Waters. (PRICE *returns to his canvas bag, kneels
to take something from it.*)

WATERS. How old are you?

PRICE. What?

WATERS. 25, 26?

PRICE. What's that gotta . . .

WATERS. What the fuck do you know about hate?
Do you know anything at *all* about it?

PRICE. Enough. I know what it's *for?*

WATERS. Do you? Listen. Before you were born . . .
you wanna know where the hate went, I'll tell you anyway, because I want you to see it . . . I was touring
with ENSA just after the war, Germany, BAOR, fool-
ing about till we got our blighty bonds. There was a
guided tour of a bit of East Germany on offer, I got
a ticket, something to do. They took us to Dresden.
Dresden? Twenty five miles of rubble. Freddie Tarle-
ton was with us, good comic, said it reminded him of
Manchester. Then they took us to another place
called Weimar, where Mozart stopped once. Mozart?
And down the road a bit we pulled up at this camp.
There was a party of schoolkids getting down off a
truck ahead of us, we followed 'em in, and over the
gate it said "To each his own." They'd turned it into
a sort of museum, each room with its special collection.
Showers in one, cyanide pellets on a table; incinerators,
with a big proud maker's label moulded in the middle,
someone in Hamburg . . . And then this . . . extraor-

dinary thing . . . in this hell-place, a special block, Der Straf-block, Punishment Block—It took a minute to register, I almost laughed, it seemed so ludicrous . . . and yet it made total sense. It was a world like any other, like ours back home. It was a world built on hate. It was just the logic of our world . . . extended. (*Pause. He stares at* PRICE, *who stays with his bag, unyielding.*) There was more . . . (*Leaving it.*) Any road. We crossed back into West Germany and we're doing a concert in Beilefeld or somewhere, Freddie's up there getting his laughs, and he tells this joke about a jew:

Heime, I lost my wallet

Have you looked in your pockets?

All but the left hip pocket

Well why don't you look in det one?

Because if I did, & it wasn't there, I'd drop dead.

People laughed, not . . . inordinately . . . And I didn't laugh. That exercise we did tonight, thinking of something deep, personal, serious, then trying to be funny about it . . . that's where it came from. And that's when I found the only jokes left were little pellets, final solutions. We're the only animal that laughs. Chimpanzees snicker, but you know what that is? Fear. They're signalling their terror. Hate. Fear. There's gotta be something better than that . . .

PRICE. What? (*Pause.*) Love, care, concern? Did you learn to love the Nazis then?

WATERS. That's not what I'm saying . . .

PRICE. Well, what then?

WATERS. It's never that simple.

PRICE. It's simple to me . . .

WATERS. That camp wasn't only repulsive . . . There was more . . .

PRICE. Like what?

WATERS. You wanna know?

PRICE. Try me.

WATERS. I got an erection. In that place. Something . . . loved it too. (*Pause. Lost.*) We've got to get deeper than hate. Hate's no help. (PRICE *stares at him for a moment, then turns away, takes two precise paces away from him. Turns.*)

PRICE. (*Almost abstractly.*) A German joke is no laughing matter.

WATERS. See it.

PRICE. (*Bridling.*) Look, *those* jews, Eddie, *those* jews . . .

WATERS. (*Lifting.*) See it!

PRICE. (*He returns to his bag, takes a book from it.*) That act I did tonight. I found it in the book you lent me. The idea.

WATERS. It was Grock. I worked with him once.

PRICE. It was Grock. Thing I liked was his . . . hardness. Not Chaplin, all coy and covered in kids. This book said he weren't even funny. He was just very truthful, in everything he did. (*He opens the book, takes out a piece of writing paper.*) I found this in another book. I brought it to show you. Some say the world will end in fire. Some say in ice. From what I've tasted of desire I hold with those who favour fire, but if I had to perish twice, I think I know enough of hate to say that for destruction ice is also great and would suffice. (*He folds the paper, puts it in his pocket, moves to desk picks up his bag, rather casually.*) It was all ice out there tonight, Eddie. I loved it. I felt . . . expressed. (*Pause. Lifting suddenly.*) *Those* Jews still stayed in line, even when they *knew*, Eddie! What's *that* about? (*He swings his bag off the desk, ready for off.*) I stand in no line. I refuse my consent. (*Pause.* WATERS *fastens his coat collar.*)

WATERS. (*Very quiet.*) What do you do now then?

PRICE. I go back. I wait. I'm ready.

WATERS. Driving, you mean?

PRICE. Driving. It doesn't matter.

WATERS. Wait for what?

PRICE. Wait for it to happen.

WATERS. (*Very low.*) Do you want help?

PRICE. No. I'm O.K. Watch out for me.

WATERS. How's Margaret?

PRICE. (*Plain.*) She left. Took the kiddie. Gone to her sister's in Bolton.

WATERS. (*Finally.*) I'm sorry.

PRICE. It's nothing. I cope. (*Pause.*) What do you do then? Carry on with this?

WATERS. I don't know.

PRICE. You should. You do it well. (*They stay a moment longer, perhaps pondering a handshake,* PRICE *turns, leaves.* WATERS *sits on at the desk, his back half turned to the door. After a moment,* PATEL *arrives, knocks on the open door.* WATERS *stands without turning.*)

WATERS. (*As though to* CARETAKER.) All right, I'm on my way . . .

PATEL. Please, I left this parcel . . .

WATERS. (*Turning, standing.*) So you did. Not been your night, has it. Me too. (PATEL *smiles, humps the sack under his arm.*) What's in there, anyway?

PATEL. Some beef. A big piece. I work at abbattoir.

WATERS. Pardon?

PATEL. Abbattoir.

WATERS. Y'eat beef do you then?

PATEL. No no, I'm Hindu. Beef, cow is sacred. This is for a friend.

WATERS. Oh (*Pause.*) Don't you mind . . . handling it?

PATEL. At first. Not now. (*He puts the sack down,*

stares around the desk.) All your funny men have gone home?

WATERS. Yeah. All the funny men have gone home.

PATEL. You like to hear a joke from my country?

WATERS. (*Frowning.*) Try me.

PATEL. (*Laughing, excited.*) It's very funny, it's very very funny. A man has many children, wife, in the South. His crop fail, he have nothing, the skin shrivel on his children's ribs, his wife's milk dries. They lie outside the house starving. All around them, the sacred cows, ten, twenty, more, eating grass. One day he take a sharp knife, mm? He creep up on a big white cow, just as he lift the knife the cow see him and the cow say: Hey, aren't you knowing you not permitted to kill me? And the man say, What do you know, a talking horse. (PATEL *laughs a lot.* WATERS *suddenly begins to laugh too.* PATEL *lifts the sack again.*)

WATERS. What do you know, a talking horse. That's Jewish. Come on, I'll give you a lift. Listen, I'm starting another class in May, why don't you join. You might enjoy it . . . (*They leave the room.* WATERS *snicks off the lights, one pair, two. The room is lit by corridor lighting only now. We hear shouted good-nights, the clanking of keys, the banging of a pair of doors. A torch light flashes into the room through the corridor window and the* CARETAKER *arrives for a final check. He flashes the light round the room. Teacher's desk, desks, dais, blackboard. The beam picks out the scrawled radiograph of* PRICE's *limerick: Hunt (cunt) etc.*)

CARETAKER. (*Finally, with considerable sourness.*) The dirty buggers.

THE END